SCARY
MOVIES

Behind the Scenes Stories, Reviews, Biographies, Anecdotes, History & Lists

A.S. Mott

**GHOST
HOUSE**

Ghost House Books

The Publisher: Ghost House Books
Distributed by Lone Pine Publishing
10145 – 81 Avenue   1808 – B Street NW, Suite 140
Edmonton, AB T6E 1W9   Auburn, WA 98001
Canada   USA

Website: http://www.ghostbooks.net
Library and Archives Canada Cataloguing in Publication

Mott, A.S. (Allan S.), 1975-
  Scary movies / A.S. Mott.
  ISBN 1-894877-70-5

  Horror films--History and criticism. I. Title.
PN1995.9.H6M67 2005   791.43'6164   C2005-902166-7

Editorial Director: Nancy Foulds
Project Editors: Carol Woo, Rachelle Delaney
Production Manager: Gene Longson
Book Design, Layout & Production: Trina Koscielnuk
Cover Design: Gerry Dotto, Curtis Pillipow

Photography Credits: Every effort has been made to accurately credit the
sources of photographs. Any errors or omissions should be directed to
the publisher for changes in future editions. Photographs courtesy of
International Communications Systems.

We acknowledge the financial support of the Government of Canada
through the Book Publishing Industry Development Program (BPIDP) for
our publishing activities.

PC: P5

Contents

Dedication

To Darren, Alison and Chris
Who have no idea they were even there.

Introduction

If my life was one of the later Godzilla movies—one of the ones where he was portrayed as a hero rather than a villain—then I suspect that the foe I would be forced to fight among the Tokyo skyline would be a rather safe and bland monster called Conventionera or maybe his even less-exciting cousin MechaTradition. It has always been my habit, when faced with a problem, to ignore the easy solution in favor of a far more laborious and potentially backbreaking alternative. Whether or not this personality quirk is self-destructive or beneficial is open to discussion amongst my friends and family, but without it, I would not have written this book, so I think I'm going to stick with it a little bit longer.

It occurred to me as I was writing this book that had I taken the traditional route to becoming a fan of the horror movie genre, I probably wouldn't have been able to write it. You see, I came to love scary movies not by watching them on television or seeing them during matinees or renting them on video,[1] but from books just like this one. Before I hit adolescence I was blessed and/or cursed with a ferocious imagination and a tremendous sense of empathy that made it impossible for me to watch any kind of horror movie, even the lame ones[2] that were only rated PG. For me, witnessing acts of bloody violence was a sure ticket to the dark streets of

---

1 Every day I am thankful to have been born just in time for the birth of the home video revolution. Whenever I think of my fellow film buffs who were forced to spend much of their lives depending on the good graces of theater owners and television programmers for access to their favorite films, I come *close* to weeping with heartfelt sympathy.

2 Whose title acronym I would later learn stood for Cannibalistic Humanoid Underground Dwellers.

Nightmare City (POP. Terror.) Yet, at the same time, in that strange way that so many people are attracted to that which repulses them, I was also fascinated by the films I could not bring myself to watch.

Every time my parents took me to the video store,[1] I would try to shore up my courage for a quick trip down the aisle that contained the horror movie section. I would hurry past its collection of frightening video covers and become both thrilled and terrified by what I saw. As I chilled out in the comedy section, I would recall the brief glimpses of the covers I had seen for movies like *Xtro* (1983), *C.H.U.D.* (1984),[2] *Terror Train* (1980), *Happy Birthday to Me* (1981) and *I Eat Your Skin* (1964), and feel compelled to learn more about them, even though I knew at that time that there was no way I could have ever sat through any one of these films.[3]

So I did what any other geeky 10-year-old would do. I went to the public library and took out every book I could find about horror movies.[4] From these books I not only learned about these films' specific plots, but also about the people who made them and why they were considered good or bad by the fans of the genre. The more I read, the more I managed to strip away the mystery of these films until I no longer feared them.

I was 11 when I watched my first scary movie all the way through without covering my eyes or leaving the room. The

---

3 And in the case of a few of these titles, when *I was* finally able to watch horror movies without running out of the room, I still couldn't sit through them, only now it was because they were so much more boring than their lurid video covers would have led anyone to believe.

4 It was in these books that I first discovered that little miracle at the bottom of the page known as the footnote. I love them, and consider them to be thoughtful gifts of bonus information. It is for this reason that I decided to use them so thoroughly in this book.

film was John McTiernan's *Predator* (1987), and from that moment on I dedicated myself to actually seeing all of the movies I had read about. It was a time full of surprises and occasional disappointments.

Many of the films were so much better than I had ever imagined them, while others were enormous letdowns. I quickly realized that many of the books I had read were written by an older generation of men[5] with different sensibilities from my own. They spoke so fondly of movies I found to be slow or stiff or unconvincing, and they dismissed newer films that I thought were much more entertaining. Perhaps it is because of this generational divide that this book is less reverent when it deals with the films of the past and more forgiving in its assessment of the films of the present. I have yet to reach the age where I am no longer impressed by anything new and try to slow the tide of my inevitable irrelevance by insisting that the films of my youth are clearly superior to all that which have since followed them.[6]

I mention this not only to help explain the book's tone,[7] but also the process that led me to choosing the six films that are discussed at length within its pages. How then did I end up picking these six films? It was easy. I picked my favorites, and I don't think it's a coincidence that five out of these six movies were all out in video stores back in the days when walking past the horror section was enough to get my heart and pulse racing.

---

5 It wouldn't be until I got to university that I found books on the subject written by women.

6 If I seemed slightly taller during this sentence, it was solely owing to the aide of the soapbox on which I was standing.

7 And its occasional statements of horror movie heresy (i.e., *The Exorcist,* 1973, sucks and a lot of remakes are just as good as the original movies they're based on).

Writing this book reminded me of that wonderful sensation, when the sight of Leatherface and his family smiling happily on the cover of *The Texas Chainsaw Massacre II* (1986) was enough to make me shiver with fearful excitement, but it also forced me to answer the question of what it is that still attracts me to these films now that I know them so well that I no longer find them frightening. Maybe some people can watch as many of these movies as I have and still retain the ability to be shocked or terrified by them, but I quickly grew immune to the horror of horror movies a long time ago.[8] So why then do I still love them?

The answer to that question came to me as I was rewatching Tim Burton's *Ed Wood* (1994) for about the 20th time. This biography about the so-called "Worst Director of All-Time"[9] isn't a scary movie by any stretch of the imagination, but in it I found the truth I had been looking for. I loved scary movies because of people like Ed Wood. Despite his reputation, Wood wasn't the worst director of all time. As a filmmaker he was incompetent to be sure, and there is no question that he lacked even the remotest smidgeon of talent, but he cared. He sincerely tried to make the kind of movies that he loved, the ones that lived inside his imagination and even though the results were unquestionably awful, they were also unique and a lot of fun to watch.

---

8 Some critics have argued that these films desensitize viewers to horror and violence, but that isn't what I'm talking about here. I long ago learned the distinction between real and pretend violence, and to this day I can be sent to Nightmare City after watching the news or a disturbing documentary, but a fictional film hasn't sent me there since I was a kid. Whenever I hear the desensitizing argument I am reminded of a quote from Canadian horror movie director David Cronenberg, "Censors tend to do what only psychopaths do: they confuse reality with illusion."

9 A designation given to him by the Medved brothers, Michael and Harry, in the sequel to their book *The Golden Turkey Awards*.

It is this quality of sincerity that permeates throughout the horror movie genre that I love above all else. The majority of the men and women who work in the genre do so not because they think it will make them rich (it usually won't) or because they think it'll allow them to eventually work on more traditional Hollywood movies (which is unlikely), but simply because they want to make movies. And like many other fans of scary movies, I would rather watch a cheap, badly made film by people who really cared about what they were doing than a much more expensive and professionally made film produced by folks whose only concern is the size of their next paycheck.

Each one of these six films, whether they were directed by talented newcomers like John Carpenter or Sam Raimi, established professionals like John Landis, Wes Craven or David Cronenberg or a Hollywood icon like Alfred Hitchcock, were made by people who truly cared about what they were doing and who strove to create projects that were unlike anything the world had ever seen before. These six men are all in some part responsible for how horror films are made today, a fact which serves as proof that nothing is more inspirational than creativity fueled by passion.

Chances are you have some opinions of your own about many of the films that I mention in this book, and you will doubtlessly disagree at some point with my views on them, be they positive or negative. That's to be expected, as there are few things more personal than how we respond to art and entertainment. I do not intend for this book to be taken as a message written in stone. The mistake so many writers make when writing about film is to assume that a personal opinion is a universal truth, and as a result they give their words an authority you seldom see outside of religious texts.

I'm not saying I won't occasionally make this same error, but when I do, please remember that mine is simply an educated opinion and not the law of the cinematic landscape.

It is also because of the personal way that people respond to these films that I have decided to not even attempt to answer the one question I know I'm going to be asked most of all once this book is finished: Why do people like scary movies? Not being a doctor in any of the relevant-logies, I don't feel that I have any right to speak for anyone else on this subject other than myself. I've already explained why I love them, but mine is not the only answer. I do think however that despite my unwillingness to state why these films remain so popular and successful today, there is enough information in this book for you to come to your own conclusions on the subject. I hope you have fun finding them.

A.S. Mott

1
Janet's
Last
Shower

Psycho

Marion Crane was a good woman
who did a very bad thing.

Knowing that the only way she could marry her boyfriend
was to get him out of debt,
she stole $40,000 from her boss.

Guilt-ridden and on the lam,
she stopped at a lonely motel along the highway.

There she met Norman Bates,
the young man who ran the place.

He lived there with his domineering mother,
Mrs. Bates,
in the gothic home behind the motel.

He seemed nice,
if just a bit shy and awkward.

Marion had no idea that he would soon be spying on her
as she undressed in her newly rented room.

And she would never ever guess that old Mrs. Bates
would be twisted enough to blame her
for Norman's voyeuristic crime
and deliver unto her
the ultimate punishment possible...

A New Kind of Horror

It's true that I don't take showers.
— Janet Leigh, *Psycho: Behind the Scenes of a Classic Thriller*

Just before I started writing this chapter on Alfred Hitchcock's *Psycho* (1990), I found myself browsing in a local bookstore, looking for any new movie-related titles that might catch my interest. As I scanned the covers in front of me, I was met by the famous image of Janet Leigh screaming in the shower not once, but twice. At first glance I had assumed I had seen two copies of the same book, but further inspection revealed that the pictures were slightly different and appeared on two competing titles. Neither book was about *Psycho*, but both were instead collections of reviews and essays about the most important films in cinematic history.

If it wasn't clear to me before just how highly regarded Hitchcock's revolutionary little thriller was, it was at that moment. The famous image chosen to illustrate the all-time greatest movies on not one, but two books was from *Psycho*, a low-budget film shot by a television crew, not *Citizen Kane* (1941) or *Gone with the Wind* (1939) or any other highly regarded classic.

It is hard for me, when I think about *Psycho*, not to feel a bit cheated. When I was born, 15 years after its release, it was already a classic whose every aspect was firmly entrenched in pop culture. Even before I became interested in scary movies, I knew about the famous shower scene and who Norman Bates was and I could easily recreate vocally the stinging shrieks of Bernard Herrmann's famous score.[1] I was robbed of the opportunity to experience *Psycho* as something completely new and unexpected. I never got a chance to appreciate firsthand just how truly revolutionary this film was and see how its influence would slowly change not only what people could see in films, but how they saw them in the theaters. I never got to gasp at the unexpected shock of seeing the film's biggest star, who I had assumed was the main character, get killed only a third of the way into the movie. I never got to watch as the teen heartthrob Anthony Perkins completely reinvented his image with the greatest performance of his career,[2] and I never got to feel the thrill of discovering that Mrs. Bates was dead and it was Norman who had been killing everyone all along.

By the time I first saw the film, two of its three sequels had already been released. The film's shocks and twists were so well known that they weren't shocking at all. They were inevitable. I knew Janet Leigh better as the mother of Jamie Lee Curtis than I did as an actress, so seeing her killed off so early didn't seem like a big deal. Anyway, that trick had already been copied by Brian De Palma in *Dressed to Kill* (1980) and would later be used by Wes Craven in *Scream* (1996), so by then it had lost its wicked flavor. Anthony Perkins had spent years typecast in B-movies and it wouldn't be until after he died that I learned that the promising career he once had had been sidetracked by audience expectations and Hollywood's refusal to see him as anything other than the boyish maniac he played to perfection.

---

1 Whose performance was always accompanied by a raised arm stabbing motion.

2 The one that would also sadly haunt him for the rest of his life.

When I sit down and watch *Psycho,* something I have done many times, I have to pretend to be someone else—a curious moviegoer in 1960 who spent hours in line just to see what it is that has got people so worked up about this latest Hitchcock picture. This doesn't work, of course, but it says something about how good the movie is—it never fails to entertain. I may have never gotten the chance to experience *Psycho* as something completely new, but that does not stop me from appreciating how truly great the film is. This is not the case with all of the scary movie classics I have seen. For example, I have never been able to enjoy Tod Browning's static and talky *Dracula* (1931) or William Friedkin's *The Exorcist* (1973), both of which were huge hits when they came out because of the way that they shocked their first audiences. And though those films' reputations both remain highly vaunted thanks to how they affected audiences when they

How Janet Leigh became a Hollywood star is one of those stories that sounds like the work of a studio publicity flack, but turns out to actually be true. When retired actress Norma Shearer saw a picture of a beautiful girl on the front desk of the hotel she was staying at, she asked the owner who the lovely young woman was. He told her it was his daughter, Jeannette, whereupon she asked him for a photograph she could take with her. A few months later Jeannette received a call from a producer friend of Shearer's who had seen the picture and asked her to appear in a screen test. Jeannette agreed and at the age of 20 and with no previous acting appearance, Jeannette was cast opposite musical star Van Johnson in *The Romance of Rosy Ridge* (1947). The studio changed her name to Janet and gave her the surname of Leigh and a star was born.

were first released, to see them now is to be disappointed. However, *Psycho* does not suffer from this problem. Instead, it only gets better with each subsequent viewing. Even after seeing it a dozen times, the prospect of watching it again elicits excitement rather than a feeling of dour obligation.

It has been called the first modern horror movie, and though one could argue and quibble over this, it is impossible to argue that it was the film that freed the genre from the traditional tales of inhuman monsters and gothic mysteries. It was the film that first played with our notions of villainy, as its insane protagonist was presented as a sympathetic character to be pitied rather than feared. The film's monster is not a madman with a butcher knife, but rather the mental illness that compels him to commit his awful crimes. *Psycho* took the horror movie out of the realm of good and evil and into a darker, grayer area. Marion Crane is a highly sympathetic character, but she's also a thief who has stolen $40,000. Norman Bates is a murderer, but he commits his crimes for the love of his mother.

But the film did more than break thematic taboos, it broke actual taboos. As hard as it may be to believe, *Psycho* contains Hollywood's first glimpse of a functioning toilet. That's not a joke. Prior to 1960, studio executives were so concerned about offending the tender sensibilities of their audiences that on-screen bathrooms were not allowed to contain toilets, for fear it might—*gasp*—remind people of what they were used for.[3]

---

3 In interviews and in her writings, Janet Leigh often argued that what made *Psycho* a superior film was that it came from a time when censorship forced filmmakers to use suggestion and innuendo to get their more explicit points across. This argument implicitly suggests that censorship was a blessing rather than a curse, a statement that I very highly doubt most filmmakers who worked in that era would support. You just have to take a look at the films Hitchcock made after *Psycho*, especially *The Birds* (1963) and *Frenzy* (1972), to see that he was more than willing to abandon his famous "restraint" once the censors at the Hayes office were stripped of all their power.

Screenwriter Joseph Stefano was so annoyed by this absurd reasoning that—with Hitchcock's permission—he deliberately made the toilet a part of *Psycho*'s plot, so he could argue to the censors that it could not be removed without damaging the film. They bought his argument and a rather strange footnote in film history was made.

The film also gave birth to a new genre of films that dealt with the completely human horror of madness and murder: the serial killer thriller. At first there were cheap *Psycho* knockoffs such as William Castle's *Homicidal* (1961) and *Strait-Jacket* (1964)[4] or Francis Ford Coppola's *Dementia 13* (1963), then more polished films such as Richard Fleischer's *The Boston Strangler* (1968), Peter Bogdanovich's *Targets* (1968) and Alan J. Pacula's *Klute* (1971). The genre reached its zenith with the success of Jonathan Demme's *The Silence of the Lambs* (1991), a film which came 31 years after *Psycho*, but which used many of its same tricks and was partly inspired by the same grisly true story of a lonely farmer who once lived in Wisconsin.

This lonely farmer inspired a lot movies over the years, so to tell the story of how *Psycho* came to be made, let's start with the sick tale of Ed Gein.

How It Happened

When Arthur Schley, the sheriff of the small town of Plainfield, Wisconsin, drove onto the Gein farm one

---

4 Whose screenplay was written by Robert Bloch, the author of the book on which *Psycho* was based.

November day in 1957, he had no idea he was about to discover one of the most horrific crime scenes in the state's history.

He and his men were there to investigate a local robbery, which they suspected had something to do with the disappearance of Bernice Worden, a hardware store owner who happened to be the mother of Sheriff Schley's deputy, Frank Worden. Ed Gein, the 51-year-old bachelor who owned the property, was considered a suspect in the robbery after having been identified as the last customer seen inside the store before Worden had gone missing. He was known around the small town as a quiet man, who seldom—if ever—socialized with others.

Inside the small farmhouse, they discovered the grisly sight of a gutted carcass hanging in the kitchen. At first they assumed it belonged to a deer, but a closer inspection revealed the horrifying truth. It was human. It was Bernice Worden. This was only the beginning of the horrors that were found inside the house. The sheriff and his deputies discovered bowls made out of skulls, collections of various body parts and—most chillingly—clothing made out of human skin.

To amass this collection Gein had resorted to both grave robbery and murder, his victims inevitably being older matronly women who reminded him of his beloved mother, a fanatically religious woman whose uncompromising war against sin had driven her son insane. He was deemed too mentally incompetent to stand trial for murder, and was instead committed to the Central State Hospital in Waupan, where he lived until he died in 1984.

As the details of Gein's crimes slowly leaked out to the rest of the world, they were noted with interest by a novelist and short story writer named Robert Bloch, who—at that time—lived not too far away from the crime scene. Bloch knew that a book could be written about the case, but he decided to fictionalize the story and tone down some of its more gruesome details. Instead of being a handyman who lived on a farm, like Gein, his main character, Norman Bates, owned and operated a small roadside motel. In the book, Norman was described as being a large, heavy man, who committed his crimes during the dark haze of his frequent alcoholic blackouts. Bloch gave the book a simple and direct title, *Psycho*.

As Bloch's book hit the shelves, Alfred Hitchcock was finishing up post-production on his latest movie, a big-budget thriller starring Cary Grant called *North by Northwest* (1959). Hitchcock had, by that point, directed over 50 films, including the Best Picture Oscar winner *Rebecca* (1940) and the suspense classics *Notorious* (1946), *Strangers on a Train* (1951), *Dial M for Murder* (1954), *Rear Window* (1954) and *Vertigo* (1958), but despite his many successes as a filmmaker, he was best known to the public as the host of the popular mystery anthology TV series *Alfred Hitchcock Presents*.[5] It was thanks to his weekly appearances on the show that bore his name that Hitchcock became the first non-acting director[6] who was truly as famous as the movie stars who appeared in his films.

Thanks to his fame and the great success of his films, Hitchcock was free to pursue any project that he desired,

---

5 The show ran for 10 years from 1955 to 1965, switching between the CBS and NBC networks several times during that time. Twenty years later, in 1985 (five years after Hitchcock's death at the age of 80), NBC ran a new version of the series for a season, using colorized introductions Hitchcock had shot for the original series.

6 Brief cameos in his own films and playing himself on TV not being enough to qualify him for actor status.

and as a follow-up to the very expensive *North by Northwest*, he decided to make another very expensive picture. As the Cary Grant film was nearing completion, Hitchcock started preparations for *No Bail for the Judge*, a thriller about a respectable British judge who wakes up one morning and discovers a murdered prostitute lying beside him. Audrey Hepburn was slated to star as the judge's daughter, a trial attorney who is joined by a suave thief, to be played by Laurence Harvey, in her attempt to prove her father's innocence. Hitchcock was about to leave Los Angeles to go to London to scout locations for the film when he noticed a copy of Bloch's book in an airport bookstore. This wasn't his first encounter with *Psycho*. He had read about it several months earlier when it received a rave review in the *New York Times Book Review*, and he had attempted to find out if there had been any studio coverage[7] on it.

Paramount, the studio that Hitchcock's production company was contracted to at the time, had done coverage on *Psycho* and had determined that it was a very interesting book, but its subject matter would make it impossible to film. This judgment went unheeded by Hitchcock, since— for reasons no one can explain—the book's coverage was never sent to him. Still busy on *North by Northwest*, Hitchcock had forgotten about his initial interest in *Psycho* until he saw the book at the airport. He bought a copy and read it on the airplane. By the time he reached London, he had decided it would make a great movie and he called his

---

7 Often before a book went out to bookstores it would be sent to the studios that hired people to read the manuscripts to decide whether or not they could become successful films. These critical judgments were—and still are to this day—referred to as coverage.

assistant, Peggy Robertson, and told her to buy the rights to it as soon as possible.[8]

Hitchcock's decision to adapt *Psycho* for the screen proved fortuitous when Audrey Hepburn decided to drop out of *No Bail for the Judge* because of her objection to a scene in which her character was to be dragged into Hyde Park and sexually assaulted. Without a star, the production was halted, and Hitchcock needed to start work on another film right away. Like all directors of his stature, he had several projects in the pipeline at all times, but he decided that he wanted to make a much lower-budgeted film than his most recent productions. This alone made *Psycho* his best bet.

A writer named James Cavanaugh, who had written several episodes of *Alfred Hitchcock Presents*, was hired to write a treatment[9] for a *Psycho* screenplay, and both Hitchcock and Robertson were amazed at how he was able to take a thrilling story and turn it into a complete snooze in just a few pages. He was fired and the search for another screenwriter began.

When Joseph Stefano walked into Hitchcock's office, he had two things going against him. He was—compared to the kind of writers Hitchcock usually worked with—relatively inexperienced, and Hitchcock had not liked the two previous films[10] that he had written, but Stefano was certain that he had an idea that would get the famous director's attention.

Stefano proposed to Hitchcock that the film should start in a hotel room where a man and a woman are meeting for a

---

8 Bloch received just $9000 for the film rights to *Psycho* and was never further compensated, even after the film's enormous success. Sadly, this isn't that different from how authors are treated by Hollywood today.

9 Often before a screenplay is written, a writer will be asked to write a treatment, which is essentially a short description of the film's plot without any dialogue.

lunchtime rendezvous. The woman wants to marry the man, but he refuses to propose to her until his financial difficulties are settled. With this on her mind, she returns back to work, where her boss entrusts her with $40,000, which she is supposed to take to a local bank. Sensing that this is her only chance at happiness, she steals the money and leaves town to take it to her lover. Along the way she is racked with guilt over her crime, while at the same time compelled to continue forward. As night falls, she decides to stop at a nearby roadside motel and rent a room for the evening. In her room, she thinks hard about the consequence of her actions and she finally concludes that they aren't worth it and decides to return the stolen money in the morning. Wanting to feel cleansed, she steps into the shower and starts washing away her guilt, but her absolution is cut short when a stranger enters the bathroom yielding a very large knife and murders her.

Stefano knew that what he was proposing was extremely audacious, as it involved totally misdirecting the audience for the first third of the movie in order to deliver a twist they would never see coming. He waited in his chair as Hitchcock pondered the consequences of such a dastardly trick. Stefano knew he had gotten the job when the director finally smiled, leaned forward and said with an almost malevolent glee, "We'll get a star to play the girl."

Hitchcock's decision to hire Stefano was probably the most important one he made on the film, as the 37-year-old

---

10 *The Black Orchid* (1958) was a melodrama starring Sophia Loren and Anthony Quinn, and *Anna of Brooklyn* (1958) was an Italian comedy starring Gina Lollobrigida that had been co-written by three other writers. At the time his most recently produced script was a teleplay entitled *The Young Juggler*, which he had written for NBC's *Ford Startime* dramatic anthology series in 1959. It coincidentally starred Tony Curtis, who was married to *Psycho*'s eventual leading lady, Janet Leigh.

screenwriter was able to bring his own experiences to the script in ways that would immediately make it more than a simple thriller. Stefano had been in psychoanalysis for some time by that point and was more sensitive than most of the psychological realities that the film was dealing with. Like Norman, he had dealt with issues regarding his mother for much of his life, but had luckily avoided any similar psychosis. It was because of this that he wanted to make Norman a sympathetic character and not just a knife-toting maniac. He struggled with replicating the character as he had appeared in the book. Bloch's Norman Bates was a large, oafish pig of a man, and definitely not someone who people could sympathize with. Stefano wanted to make Norman younger and a lot less despicable. On this point, the famous director was ahead of him. He too had been thinking about who in Hollywood would be capable of invoking both qualities of psychosis and innocence at the same time. The answer was obvious.

Before appearing in *Psycho*, Anthony Perkins had a reputation for playing extremely conflicted characters. In *Friendly Persuasion* (1956)[11] for example, he played a young Quaker who rebels against his parents and his upbringing to join the Union army during the Civil War, and in *Fear Strikes Out* (1957) he played Jimmy Piersall, a real-life baseball player

---

11 For which he would receive his only Oscar nomination.

12 While I do not want to delve into any kind of psychoanalytic theorizing about Perkins' strange on-screen charisma, it isn't hard to deduce that it must have been influenced by the fact that he was a gay man living in a time where his sexuality was considered unspeakable.

13 Originally named Mary in both the book and the script, the character's name was changed when the studio legal department located a woman named Mary Crane who lived in the area where the story took place.

whose relationship with his overbearing father led him to having a nervous breakdown. Even in less dramatic films such as *Green Mansions* (1958), *The Matchmaker* (1958) and *Tall Story* (1960), he projected a quality of neurosis that served as sharp contrast to his handsome, boyish features. His apparent fragility only made him that much more likable, and directors who wanted someone more complex than the era's typical leading men[12] used it to good effect. He was perfect for Hitchcock and Stefano's reinvented Norman Bates.

For the part of Marion Crane,[13] Hitchcock was true to his word and cast a star. Known for his preference for blondes, Hitchcock offered the role to Janet Leigh, who—at 33—was considered a member of Hollywood royalty thanks to her marriage to screen idol Tony Curtis and her charming performances in 33 movies over the past 13 years. Best known for appearing in lighthearted fare such as *Houdini* (1953), *Prince Valiant* (1954) and *My Sister Eileen* (1955), she had also experimented with roles in grittier films such as *Rogue Cop* (1954) and Orson Welles' *Touch of Evil* (1958), which meant she wasn't afraid of dealing with *Psycho*'s controversial subject matter. Thrilled both by the chance to work with

Much has been written about Hitchcock's relationships with his female leading ladies. Despite being extremely devoted to his wife Alma, who was very supportive throughout his career, he became infatuated with many of the beautiful women he worked with, most famously Ingrid Bergman, Grace Kelly and Tippi Hedren. In one of his most famous acts of malice, he sent a young Melanie Griffith, Tippi Hedren's daughter, a doll made up to look like her mother lying inside of a coffin-shaped box.

Hitchcock and the complexity of the role, she had no qualms whatsoever about the fact that her character only appeared in the first third of the movie or that it would require her to appear virtually naked on-screen. But as excited as she was, there was no way she could have ever known just how important her small role would become in the annals of movie history.

For the part of Sam Loomis, Marion's lover, Hitchcock decided to cast a more conventional leading man and chose John Gavin, a Rock Hudson clone whose acting career never amounted to much before or after his performance in *Psycho*.[14] The part of Lila Crane, Marion's concerned sister, was given to Vera Miles, an actress Hitchcock had once intended to groom for superstardom, but when she became pregnant during preproduction on *Vertigo* (1958), she fell out of his favor. Her brief appearance in the film was simply a matter of contractual obligation. Martin Balsam, a character actor from New York, then best known for his performance as Juror #1 in *Twelve Angry Men* (1957), was cast as the investigator Milton Arbogast, and in the small role of Caroline, Marion's mousy coworker, Hitchcock cast his own daughter Patricia, who had previously appeared as the doomed and despised wife of Farley Granger in his suspense classic *Strangers on a Train* (1951).[15]

---

14 It was rumored that Hitchcock hated Gavin's performance and took to referring to the actor as "The Stiff." Thanks to another actor whose film career was mostly negligible—Ronald Reagan—Gavin was appointed as the ambassador to Mexico for a brief period during the 1980s.

15 Eagle-eyed viewers can also catch a glimpse of future sitcom star Ted Knight in the role of one of the policemen guarding Norman's cell at the end of the movie.

16 As *Psycho* had gone into production Hitchcock decided to leave Paramount and move over to Universal, which explains how that creepy house became a part of the famous studio tour.

Wanting *Psycho* to be made for as little money as possible, Hitchcock decided to film it using the same crew that produced his weekly television show. Not only were they fast, as the pace of TV production demanded, they were used to working in the black-and-white format, which has its own unique technical challenges. Apart from the scenes at the beginning of the film where Marion attempts to elude the police, most of the film was shot inside of a studio lot at Universal.[16] Hitchcock loathed working on location and avoided it whenever he could, preferring the calm predictability of a movie set to the chaotic *force majeure*s that inevitably came with shooting in a real-life setting.

The other reason Hitchcock preferred to work on set was because it allowed him to indulge in his habit of halting production each day at 6:00 PM, so he could have dinner with his wife, Alma. Working on location meant having to stay until all the required shots had been completed, while on a set it was easy to simply put everything down and pick up where filming stopped the next day. Like many meticulous directors, the joy of filmmaking for Hitchcock was in the initial preparation and planning, while the actual production itself was a chore. Hitchcock had long ago figured out a way

The shower scene was the major reason Hitchcock decided to shoot the film in black and white. He felt that if he had shot the movie in color, the blood in the scene would have been too much for the censors and the audience to handle. And, yes, the blood so famously seen circling the drain is really chocolate syrup, which the prop department had discovered looked the most realistic when combined with the water.

to help him get through the wearying obligation of filming his meticulously prepared scenarios. He did this by constantly concocting ways to challenge himself, either technically or creatively.

When he was becoming well known for the suspenseful editing of his pictures, he decided to make *Rope* (1948), which was filmed in long, uninterrupted, 10-minute takes.[17] When *Psycho* itself was praised for its extremely effective score by Bernard Herrmann, he decided to make a film, *The Birds* (1963), which had no score at all.[18] He chose to make *Lifeboat* (1944) because of the narrative challenge inherent in making a compelling drama that took place in just one very small boat. The same was true for *Rear Window* (1954), where he had to craft a suspense picture using a crippled main character who could not leave his apartment. For *Spellbound* (1945) he worked with the surrealist master Salvador Dali to help him devise nightmarish sequences intended to show the depths of Gregory Peck's madness.

Psycho was no exception to this rule. The scene in the shower was as challenging as any he would ever face. With it he needed to show the horror of violence and the vulnerability of the naked victim without showing either on camera. It was the crucial turning point of the film. If it didn't work, the whole film would be in trouble.

---

17 His follow-up to *Rope, Under Capricorn* (1949) took this use of uninterrupted takes to even more complicated levels.

18 Although Herrmann did work on the film by helping shape its use of natural bird calls into an equally ominous, if not traditionally musical, soundtrack.

19 Back when I was in university, my film professor showed the class a tape he had made of shower scenes that were directly inspired by Hitchcock's film. It was a long tape with at least 25 scenes on it. I personally contributed one more to his effort by telling him about the scene he had missed from *Monster in the Closet* (1987).

It is hard to appreciate today just how difficult a task Hitchcock had set for himself. Nowadays the only thing holding a director back when filming such a scene[19] is his or her contractual obligation to get a specific rating, but Hitchcock was working in a Hollywood where—as has been discussed earlier—his inclusion of a flushing toilet was considered groundbreaking. At that time, the sequence was unfilmable—Bloche's book concluded with Norman, dressed as his mother, decapitating his victim after brutally stabbing her with a knife. This detail was omitted from Stefano's screenplay. Smartly avoiding the risk of raising the concerns of studio censors, Stefano chose to write the sequence as simply as possible. It would be up to Hitchcock to take the moment and turn it into one of the most memorable scenes in movie history.[20]

To help him visualize the sequence, Hitchcock hired the renowned opening-title designer Saul Bass[21] to storyboard the entire sequence. In the years before his death in 1996, Bass took to telling interviewers that his involvement was such that he essentially directed the sequence himself, a claim that Janet Leigh and other crew members have strongly refuted. While Bass did create the storyboards for the shower sequence, he was never on set when the scene was filmed and had no involvement in how it was edited.

---

20 In 2004, UCI Cinemas, a British theater chain, conducted a survey to determine the top movie moment from the past 50 years. *Psycho's* shower scene easily took the top spot.

21 Bass, best known as the designer for the title sequences to films such as *Spartacus* (1960), *West Side Story* (1961) and *It's a Mad Mad Mad Mad World* (1963), was also the director of the underrated animal attack movie (the animals in this case being normal-sized—but hyper-intelligent—ants) *Phase IV* (1974).

Hitchcock took an entire week to shoot the short sequence.[22] The set was tiny, 12 feet by 12 feet, and it was supposed to be closed, meaning only the most essential crew members were allowed to be there, but Leigh couldn't help but notice wryly that there seemed to be far more electricians up on the catwalk than were actually needed. By the time the week was over, being nearly naked was the least of her concerns.

It would still be four years until Sidney Lumet pushed the boundaries of the Hayes Code[23] to the breaking point with *The Pawnbroker* (1964), which was the first mainstream Hollywood film to include undisguised nudity since the code had been established, so Hitchcock and his crew had to work very hard to make sure the shower scene was realistic without aggravating the censors. To help them out, a nude body double named Marli Renfro was hired so the crew could determine just how much water and steam was required to hide away what needed to be hidden from the camera. Before shooting had begun, Leigh and costume designer Rita Riggs had to figure out what she would wear in the scene. They finally settled on patches of moleskin, which adhered quite nicely to the body, didn't come off in the water and were virtually invisible on black and white film.

The shoot was long and tedious for everyone, as over 70 shots were filmed over the week, each one requiring unique

22 Shooting this one scene accounted for one-third of the time Leigh spent working on the picture.

23 In 1930, Hollywood executives were worried how censorship boards might affect their profits, so they adopted a universal standard of decency which all of the studios would follow. To this end the former Postmaster General, Will Hayes, was hired to enforce these new rules, which were referred to as the Hayes Code in his honor. It wouldn't be until 1966 that the Motion Picture Association of America decided to jettison the code in favor of a less restrictive ratings system directed by Jack Valenti.

lighting and camera setups, but it was Leigh who suffered the most, especially while they labored to capture the famous shot that began on her eye and moved back to reveal Marion Crane's dead body. This proved to be the most difficult shot to film in the whole movie. Not only was Leigh required to keep her eyes open for the entire shot, but she also had to make sure they were devoid of any signs of life. This alone would be hard, given how long the shot is, but it was made even more difficult by the fact that she was required to be wet and the water had a tendency to drip down into her eyes. Today this wouldn't be a problem as digital technology makes it easy to remove any inadvertent eye blinks, but back then it was all up to the actress to get it right. During one take, Leigh could feel that the piece of moleskin that was covering her backside was starting to come off and she let it; her modesty was no match for her desire to get her ordeal finished with.[24]

The time, effort and pain proved to be worth it when the sequence was complete. Together with Bernard Herrmann's famous shrieking score, Hitchcock created a scene in which, thanks to a combination of movement and montage, the violence of the act it depicted was implied without ever being made explicit. Each shot and edit served to act as a slash of the knife,[25] a technique that proved so effective that many people insisted they had seen things that simply weren't there. The

---

24 Despite her best efforts, one eye blink did make it into Hitchcock's edit of the film. Neither he nor his editor George Tomasini noticed it during preproduction, but Alma, Hitchcock's eagle-eyed wife, caught the mistake during the film's first screening.

25 In order to keep the audience from guessing the true identity of Mrs. Bates, Hitchcock decided to cast different people to play her during the film. In the shower scene it isn't Anthony Perkins who we see approach Marion through the curtain, but instead an actress named Margo Epper.

complexity of the scene, combined with its shocking place-
ment within the context of the film, made it an instant classic
and in the years that have followed, it has been endlessly imi-
tated (and parodied), but it has never been replicated.

The same could be said for the film's other piece of
bravura masterwork, Anthony Perkins' haunting lead performance. Distancing himself even more from the book than
screenwriter Stefano had intended, Perkins chose to highlight
the juvenile simplicity of Norman's nature, best exemplified
by his constant snacking on candy and his childlike fear and
devotion to his mother. By doing so he made the audience
perceive him as a pathetic victim of his own situation, which
made him sympathetic even as he spied on Marion as she
undressed[26] and when he disposed of her dead body. His performance, above anything else, was what made *Psycho* a tran-
scendent classic and not just a thriller. Every accolade the
film has ever earned leads to his performance[27] as much as it
does to Hitchcock.

But Perkins alone wasn't completely responsible for the
presence that Norman Bates has in the film. As mentioned

There is a—possibly apocryphal—story about a studio cen-
sor who objected to the scene the first time he saw it
because he was certain he had seen shots where the knife
penetrated the skin, but when he saw it a second time he
admitted that no such shots existed, but he still objected to
the scene because this time he was certain he had seen a
shot where Leigh was clearly naked. Even if this particular
story isn't true, the fact is many people who saw it were
fooled by their own imaginations into seeing much more
than they were shown.

earlier, other actors doubled for Perkins when Norman was supposed to be acting out as his dead mother and it was only when Mrs. Bates' true identity was revealed that he himself donned the dress.[28] Not only did it take several actors (and one dummy) to give the dead Mrs. Bates a body, it also took several actors to give her a voice as well. Paul Jasmin, a fashion designer and photographer for such magazines as *Vogue*, was a friend of Anthony Perkins who often entertained people with his impression of a shrewish older woman he called Eunice.[29] Hitchcock heard the impression when Perkins gave him a tape of one of Jasmin's "performances" and thought it was perfect for the part, but that it wouldn't work all by itself. Two actresses, Virginia Gregg and Jeanette Nolan, were also hired to record all of Mrs. Bates' dialogue. Hitchcock then had his sound department take the three different recordings and splice them together, sometimes going so far as to use all three for one simple line of dialogue. It was only in the film's final scene, where Mrs. Bates performs a monologue while her son sits motionless in his jail cell, that Hitchcock relied mostly on one actress, in this case Gregg, who would be the only one of the three to return to the part in the subsequent sequels.

---

26 The painting that Norman uses to hide the hole in the wall is a depiction of "Susanna and Her Elders," which is a story that combines voyeurism with violence.

27 Among these honors, the American Film Institute named *Psycho* the greatest thriller of all time and ranked Norman Bates second in its list of the top 50 movie villains of all time. The top spot went to Anthony Hopkins for his portrayal of Hannibal Lecter in *Silence of the Lambs* (1991). Personally I think the ranking positions should have been reversed.

28 Hitchcock originally intended Norman's sudden appearance in drag to play out without music, but the moment came across as flat and anti-climatic. It was composer Bernard Herrmann who suggested that the scene would be more effective with a repetition of the disturbing music that had been heard during Marion's murder.

29 To the amusement of such well-known friends as Stanley Kubrick and Broadway actress Elaine Stritch, he would use the voice to harass unsuspecting celebrities over the phone.

If Janet Leigh's final moment in the shower scene was the most difficult shot for Hitchcock and his crew to get, the scene where Lila Crane discovers that old Mrs. Bates ain't quite as alive as the audience has thus far presumed also proved to be a challenge.[30] The shot Hitchcock had envisioned was extremely complicated and required a tightly choreographed crew in order to get it filmed. In the scene, Vera Miles (as Lili) was supposed to touch Mrs. Bates on the shoulder, causing her chair to turn around, which would then cause Vera to scream and fling her arm back, hitting the naked light bulb above her and causing it to swing back and forth as the taxidermic corpse is revealed. What really made this difficult was Hitchcock's insistence that a flare of light hit the camera as Mrs. Bates' dead body is revealed. To do this, a prop man had to kneel below the camera's view and turn the chair at the same time that Vera hit the light bulb in order to sync with the movement of the camera. As each attempt at the shot failed, Hitchcock began to get angrier and angrier, and when he watched the dailies and saw that nothing they had shot that day came close to what he wanted, he lost his temper, something he very rarely did. The crew was finally able to make it happen on the second day of shooting.

Filming on *Psycho* ended on the first day of February 1960 and ended up costing just $800,000. Before they finished,

---

30 Ironically the shot that *looks* like it would have been the hardest to achieve, where Martin Balsam's character, Milton Arbogast, falls backward down the stairs after being stabbed, was actually quite simple to pull off. Balsam merely stood in front of some pre-filmed projected footage of the camera going down the stairs and acted as though he was tumbling backwards.

31 Sadly, this technique is shunned by today's studio marketers, who insist that every single plot point be revealed in the trailer. Even sadder is the fact that research has proven that many moviegoers, particularly men, are reluctant to go to a movie if they aren't fully aware of what it is all about.

Hitchcock had taken the unusual step of filming a trailer for the film, which featured him giving the audience a tour of the film's sets while making jokes and dropping hints about what they could expect to see in the movie. By this time, the rotund director had become so famous that—with all apologies to his talented actors—he was the real star of his films and it made sense to market the film as being an Alfred Hitchcock production rather than to sell it on the appeal of Anthony Perkins and Janet Leigh. But this wasn't the trailer's only purpose. By focusing on Hitchcock, he and the studio were able to advertise the picture without actually showing any scenes from it, thus ensuring that none of the film's surprises would be spoiled.[31] They even went so far as to include, at the very end of the trailer, a shot of Vera Miles standing and screaming inside the shower, suggesting that she, and not Janet Leigh, was the victim. As innovative as this was, it didn't even come close to the gimmick that Hitchcock had planned for when the movie was released to theaters. It was a plan that not only made his film a national sensation, but also changed the way all movies would eventually be exhibited.

The Aftermath

As soon as Hitchcock started working on *Psycho,* he grew increasingly concerned with a potential problem that might limit the movie's success. Knowing that one of the film's biggest draws would be the shocking murder of the lead actress, which was just a third of the way through the picture, he was concerned that the scene's effect would be greatly lessened by the way theaters screened movies at that time. In those days, movie theaters showed their movies repeatedly all throughout the day, and it was quite common for members of the audience to come in during the middle of a movie and stay in their seat until the next showing and watch what they had missed the first time around. Hitchcock knew that if people came into the theater after the shower scene, the effect of the film would be lost on them, so he decided to take the very unusual step of forcing all of the movie theaters that showed *Psycho* to refuse anyone admittance into the theater once the movie had begun. Theater owners protested this ultimatum vehemently, insisting that such a move would cost them customers, but Hitchcock—with the studio's backing—held firm.

Cardboard stand-ups that featured Hitchcock explaining *Psycho*'s unique admittance policy were distributed to all of the theaters showing the film, which helped to create a buzz among the public, as they wondered what possible reason the famous director could have to insist on such a rule. Also featured on the stand-ups was a request from Hitchcock that all of the people who saw the film kept its shocking twists to themselves, so as not to spoil it for the uninitiated. This made people even more curious about the film, as they wanted to know what could possibly be so shocking about the film that Hitchcock would want to enlist their service in keeping it a secret.[32] Long lines formed at every theater showing the film

---

32 Over the years several other films have been successful in employing this strategy to promote their films. *The Crying Game* (1992), *The Usual Suspects* (1995) and *The Sixth Sense* (1999) all worked at the box office because audiences were delighted to send unsuspecting friends and family to see a movie with a twist they knew they would not see coming.

33 And it changed how many movie theaters perceived their industry. Where once they were in the business of selling tickets to simply gain entrance into their theaters, they—following the massive success of Hitchcock's experimental admittance policy—realized that they could instead charge people per screening, which is, of course, the industry standard today.

the day it opened. If the theater owners were once reluctant to follow Hitchcock's rule, they now adopted it almost religiously. Reporters were sent from various newspapers to see if they could bribe or sneak their way into a screening after it had started and they were all thwarted. One reporter even went so far as to bring a pregnant woman with him to a theater and request that she be allowed into the theater so she wouldn't have to stand in line until the next showing. The theater manager refused to let her in, but did offer to let her sit down in his office until the next showing began.

Hitchcock's policy and his request for secrecy was easily understood by everyone who saw the film. As I described above, I can only imagine what it must have been like to first see *Psycho* without having any clue as to what it was about, but the sensation must have been intensely thrilling.

The filmed earned over $40 million at the box office,[33] a phenomenal amount in 1960, especially for a low-budget black and white film. It also proved to be a hit with the critics, earning nearly universal raves, with the exception of a few pans from older, more conservative, critics who were disgusted by the film's unusual amount of violence. When Hollywood's annual awards season began, the film earned four Oscar nominations for Best Director, Best Supporting Actress, Best Black and White Cinematography[34] and Best Black and White Art Direction.[35] They all lost.[36] What's most

34 John L. Russell in a category that obviously no longer exists today.

35 Joseph Hurley, Robert Clatworthy and George Milo.

36 Billy Wilder won Best Director for *The Apartment* (1960), which also won for best picture. Janet Leigh was beat out by Shirley Jones for her performance in *Elmer Gantry* (1960). Freddie Francis won for his black and white photography of *Sons and Lovers* (1960) and Alexandre Trauner and Edward G. Boyle won for their set direction of *The Apartment*. This proved to be Hitchcock's sixth and final nomination for Best Director, which he infamously never won.

shocking about this are the obvious omissions. As good as the film is it is easy to understand why the Academy members would be reluctant to nominate it for Best Picture, but it is almost impossible to accept that neither Anthony Perkins nor Joseph Stefano were nominated for their work on the film. Perkins' snub is especially troubling, considering how truly iconic his performance has proven to be. It doesn't help that time has not been kind to the performances that did receive nominations. Laurence Olivier's turn in *The Entertainer* (1960) now seems overly theatrical; Trevor Howard's performance in *Sons and Lovers* (1960) is decent, but the film itself has been long forgotten; Spencer Tracy is good in *Inherit the Wind* (1960), but it's fairly obvious he was nominated more out of affection than merit; and the winner, Burt Lancaster, for *Elmer Gantry* (1960), delivers a performance that now seems dated to most present viewers. Of the five nominees, only Jack Lemmon in *The Apartment* (1960) comes close to matching Perkins' achievement. It's likely that the same prejudice against horror movies that kept *Psycho* from being nominated for Best Picture contributed to Perkins' lack of recognition, which is truly unfortunate given that the role had typecasted him for the rest of his career, and he never come close to a role that great again.

Like many actors who hit such a powerful chord with audiences with a certain role, Perkins soon found that people had difficulty seeing him as anything other than Norman Bates. Following the success of *Psycho* he had to go to Europe to find work in a series of international productions that did little to further his career. In 1968 he returned to *Psycho* territory with a role in *Pretty Poison* where he played a disturbed young man whose life is ruined by his infatuation with a beautiful but sociopathic woman played by Tuesday Weld. In the 1970s he had to make do with small supporting roles in box office disasters such as *Catch-22* (1970), *Lovin' Molly* (1974), *Mahogany* (1975) and *The Black Hole* (1979), with only the occasional bright spots of *The Life and Times of Judge Roy Bean* (1972), *Murder On the Orient Express* (1974) and *Winter Kills* (1979) to redeem him. In 1973, he collaborated with famed Broadway composer Stephen Sondheim on the screenplay for a murder mystery entitled *The Last of Sheila* (1973), and the result was one of the most entertaining puzzle films of that decade, but—for whatever reason—the two of them chose to not follow it up with another script.

By 1983, Alfred Hitchcock had been dead for three years and his films were still looked upon with great affection by the public. The most popular of his films was still *Psycho* and its continued presence in the public's psyche gave some people in Hollywood a daring idea. It seemed almost blasphemous to propose making a sequel to such a classic, but the heretics in Tinseltown greeted the idea with a bagful of cash. Tom Holland[37] was hired by producers Hilton A. Green[38] and Bernard Schwartz to write a screenplay that imagined what would happen if Norman Bates was released from the insane asylum he had been in since the end of the first film and returned to the Bates Motel. An Australian named Richard Franklin who had previously made a thriller starring Jamie Leigh Curtis called *Roadgames* (1981) and a "comedic" softcore film called *Fantasm* (1976) was hired to direct. As angry

---

37 Who had written the screenplays for *The Beast Within* (1982) and the revenge thriller *Class of 1984* (1982) and who would later go on to write and direct the classic 1980s vampire film *Fright Night* (1985).

38 Who worked as the assistant director on the first film.

as he was by how his most famous role had sidetracked his once-promising career, Anthony Perkins saw the benefits that could come with once again playing Norman and agreed to make the film.

The resulting film did a disservice to the original, but it wasn't quite bad enough to earn any feelings of enmity from its audience. Its final twist, in which the woman who had turned Norman into a maniac turned out not to be his real mother, had none of the startling power of the first film's climatic reveal. Still, the film did well enough to merit another sequel, which came three years later. Perkins decided that if he was going to play Norman again, he might as well get something more than a paycheck out of it, so he demanded that he be allowed to direct the movie. The result was a far more entertaining film than its rather low rating on the Internet Movie Database would suggest. Perkins gave the film the same kind of campy humor that had made his screenplay for *The Last of Sheila* so enjoyable. While certainly not in the same league as the original, it is easily one of the best of the many slasher movies that were made during that decade.[39]

A year later the franchise took a strange detour into television when NBC aired a television movie called *Bates Motel* (1987). Intended to be a pilot for a possible series, the movie starred Bud Cort[40] as Alex West, a man in his 30s who has spent the past 27 years in an insane asylum after killing his

---

39 Perkins would only make one more movie as a director. *Lucky Stiff* (1988) was a fun, black comedy about an overweight man who discovers that his gorgeous blond girlfriend is only dating him so she can take him home to her family and serve him as their Christmas dinner. It received almost no theatrical distribution and was eventually released on video, but like *Psycho III*, it proved that Perkins had a John Waters-like sensibility that could have gone to greater things had he been given the chance.

40 Immortalized forever as Harold in the classic *Harold and Maude* (1971).

abusive father when he was a child. There in the asylum, he met a fellow patient named Norman, who became Alex's friend and mentor. When Norman died, he left Alex the motel he still owned in Arizona. Now free, Alex claims the Bates Motel with the intention of opening it back up for business, only to discover that it is a place where strange things seem to happen. Ratings weren't good and the series was never picked up, but if it had, it appears that the show would have been something like a supernatural *Love Boat* where the plots would focus on the odd things that happened to the guests who stayed there.

Four years after *Psycho III*, Perkins played Norman one last time in the made-for-cable *Psycho IV: The Beginning* (1990). In the movie, which was written by Joseph Stefano and directed by Mick Garris,[41] Norman finds himself tormented by memories of his relationship with his mother, as he becomes a regular caller on a late-night radio show. Most of the film consists of flashbacks, which feature Henry Thomas (Elliot in *ET: The Extra-Terrestrial* (1982)) as a young Norman and Olivia Hussey (Juliet in *Romeo and Juliet* (1968)) as an attractive Mrs. Bates. In the end, Stefano's script lacked the magic of the original and the result is the least well known of the film's three sequels.

That same year Perkins tested positive for HIV, and he learned he had the AIDS virus. He died in 1992, most likely having contracted the disease while he was working on *Psycho III*.

His death should have permanently halted the *Psycho* franchise, but then in 1998, iconoclastic director Gus Van

---

41 A genre director best known for his frequent collaborations with novelist Stephen King.

Sant shocked the world when he announced with producer Brian Grazer that he was going to follow the success of his Oscar-winning hit *Good Will Hunting* (1997) with a color, shot-for-shot recreation of Alfred Hitchcock's film. Film buffs around the world howled in protest, considering such a project to be the worst kind of cinematic sacrilege. Despite this, Van Sant was able to lure a very talented cast onto the project, including—most notably—Vince Vaughn as Norman and Anne Heche[42] as Marion. When the film was finally released it was met with almost universal disinterest and has become virtually forgotten less than a decade later.

If any good came out of Van Sant's misbegotten recreation, it was that it reminded people just how good the original was. While it is almost impossible today to understand just how shocking it must have been in 1960, we can all easily appreciate the effect it had on popular culture. This one film helped pave the way towards a more permissive film industry, took the horror movie genre in an entirely new direction and literally changed how many movie theaters did their business. For any other film, just one of these achievements would be enough to deem it important, but by pulling off the hat trick, *Psycho* earns a spot among the true all-time greats. Like *Gone with the Wind* (1939), *The Wizard of Oz* (1939) and *Citizen Kane* (1941), it has achieved a place in the public consciousness so vast that it can no longer be considered just entertainment, but instead a valuable part of our modern cultural mythology.

---

42 Years later Heche would seem to have been the better choice to play Norman when she revealed her own struggle with mental illness in her autobiography *Call Me Crazy*.

Also Look For

Your best bet for the film itself is Universal Studio's collector's edition DVD, which includes a great transfer of the film along with a very entertaining feature-length documentary about the making of the film. The first two sequels and Gus Van Sant's remake are also available on DVD, although they are much harder to find. As of this writing, *Psycho IV* is available only as an out-of-print videotape, but you might still be able to find it at your local video store. While there are rumors that *Bates Motel* was released on video years ago, I've never seen a copy and chances are most online versions you'll find are fuzzy bootlegs from its various televised airings.

If you would like to read more about the movie, you should begin with Christopher Nickens and Janet Leigh's *Psycho: Behind the Scenes of the Classic Thriller*, a short but very insightful account about the creation of the first film straight from the source. There are far too many Alfred Hitchcock biographies out there to single any out, but I do recommend that you look for two well-written biographies about Anthony Perkins that have been released since his death in 1992. Both Ronald Bergan's *Anthony Perkins: A Haunted Life* and Charles Winecoff's *Split Image: The Life of Anthony Perkins* are unvarnished accounts of the actor's life that, despite their more salacious details, honor him by reminding the reader that there was far more to this very complicated man than the tortured and bewildered murderer he had made so famous.

A Thrilling
Kind of Madness

The Good

Over the years, the psycho/serial killer film has easily become the most popular of all the scary movie sub-genres. This has a lot to do with the fact that studio publicity departments are often able to market them as police procedurals or hyper-intense mysteries rather than as horror movies. Referred to as thrillers, these films are not associated with the horror genre, which means people are much more willing to accept them as popular entertainment. The irony is that many of the people who refuse to watch a film such as *Halloween* (1978) because it is a horror film, will watch movies such as *Silence of the Lambs* (1991), dramatic TV shows such as *The Profiler*, as well as the seemingly countless true-crime serial killer documentaries that are the backbone of several popular cable channels,[1] even though these productions are—in their own way—easily as horrific as any of the more stereotypical genre offerings. That said, here are five movies that I think represent the sub-genre at its best.

1) ***Sisters*** **(1973):** Before Brian De Palma became famous for his later Hitchcockian rip-offs/homage's such as *Obsession* (1976) and *Dressed to Kill* (1980), he made this hilariously

---

1 I'm talking about you, A&E.

shocking thriller starring a young and beautiful Margot Kidder as a French-Canadian model adjusting to life in a big American city. To say any more about the film would spoil it for you, but I highly recommend that you watch it on a double bill with Frank Henenlotter's *Basket Case* (1982) and learn all about the possible dangers of becoming too close with your siblings.

2) *Targets* (1968): Taking a challenge given to him by producer Roger Corman, writer and director Peter Bogdanovich[2] managed to take scenes from a bad movie called *The Terror* (1963) along with new footage shot in two days with horror movie icon Boris Karloff, and make it into a true horror classic. Inspired by the senseless mass murder committed by Texas sniper Charles Whitman, Bogdanovich concocted a story that contrasted a day in the life of an old horror movie star named Byron Orlock, who has decided to retire from acting because his brand of terror just doesn't seem frightening anymore, and a handsome young man named Bobby Thompson, who has decided to kill his wife and parents before going out and shooting at as many innocent strangers as he can before someone stops him. And with these two contrasting plot lines, Bogdonavich shows how the fantasies we see on-screen could never be considered more horrible than the mundane realities of everyday life.

3) *Frailty* (2001): The directorial debut of well-known actor Bill Paxton,[3] *Frailty* is a small but terrifying film that asks the

---

2 Who also made the truly scary Burt Reynolds musical *At Long Last Love* (1975).

3 Whose scary movie acting credits include *Mortuary* (1983), *Aliens* (1986), *Near Dark* (1987), *Brain Dead* (1990), *Predator 2* (1990), the slasher movie satire *Club Dread* (2004) and the infamous *Boxing Helena* (1993), a psychosexual melodrama so horribly misconceived it manages to invoke a level of dread in its audience that an intentionally frightening film could never hope to replicate.

viewer what they would do if one day their beloved father came to them and said that God had sent him on a mission to kill the demons who live in our world in human form. Do you believe him even when the "demons" he brings home appear to be nice, normal people? Or do you try to stop him, even if it means having to kill him yourself? First-time screenwriter Brent Hanley manages to create a world that makes this a very difficult question to answer, and he fills his plot with the kind of twists and turns that linger with you for days after you've seen them.

4) *Henry, Portrait of a Serial Killer* **(1986):** Loosely based on the true story of a murderous drifter named Henry Lee Lucas,[4] John McNaughton's *Henry, Portrait of Serial Killer* is a difficult-to-watch cinema verite examination of a man who does not know how to live life without inflicting violence on others. As played by Michael Rooker, Henry is a shell of a man whose inability to experience pleasure or feel empathy is a direct result of the grim realities of life that have tormented him since he was a child. Like a good documentary, the film never condemns Henry or sympathizes with what he does, but rather forces us to understand how a monster like this can be created in our society. A good companion piece to go with the Aileen Wuornos docudrama *Monster* (2003), the

---

4 Lucas made a name for himself in the 1980s when he confessed to the authorities that he was responsible for over 80 murders, many of which it was later proved that he could not have committed. In the 1990s his name once again made the news when he became the only person on Texas' Death Row to receive clemency from then-governor George W. Bush. His sentence was commuted to life imprisonment when the Attorney General of Texas proved to Governor Bush that Lucas could not have killed the woman he had been given the death penalty for murdering.

film was followed by a much more typically exploitative sequel in 1998 that did not feature the involvement of anyone related to the original film and suffers greatly as a result.

5) *Seven* (1995): Chances are that of all the films mentioned in this chapter, this is the one most of you have seen. See it again. Much more than a typical buddy-cop move, *Seven* is an atmospheric and chilling example of a corrupt world where the only reward for heroism is disillusionment. Like Roman Polanski's *Chinatown* (1974), *Seven* is that rare studio film which sends us into the world that even independent filmmakers are often reluctant to explore—a place where the good are not guaranteed a victory over evil and where the insane can say things that make a horrible kind of sense. It is as brave as mainstream cinema gets.

A portrait of wrath. (Brad Pitt in *Seven*)

The Not-So-Good

The existence of these five films does serve as proof that even a film as great as *Psycho* can lead to *very* bad things.

1) *Color of Night* (1994): When director Richard Rush released *The Stunt Man* in 1980, it was hailed as a masterpiece, and though it never became a mainstream hit, many film buffs considered it one of the best films to appear during that largely cinematically desolate decade. His achievement was so great that he chose to wait 14 years before he made another film, a virtual lifetime in the fast-paced world of Hollywood. Still, his reputation was such that when he decided to make his comeback with *Color of Night*, he was able to get one of the world's biggest actors, Bruce Willis, to star in it. Almost immediately the project drew controversy when the media found out that Rush had filmed explicit sex scenes featuring a fully nude Willis with his costar Jane March.[5] But in the end, all of the fuss about Willis' nudity turned out to be (if you can forgive the phrase) much ado about nothing. Rush's comeback was a disaster, a laughably bad film whose conclusion hinged on a "shocking twist" that you literally had to be deaf and blind not to see coming within the first half-hour of the film. Even with the sex scenes heavily cut in order for the film to get an R-rating it was sadly obvious that Rush had waited all that time to give the world just another *Basic Instinct* (1992) rip-off. Luckily for Willis,

---

5 An actress who had previously earned some infamy due to her appearance in the then-scandalous, but now-forgotten erotic drama *The Lover* (1992).

this film came out the same year as *Pulp Fiction* (1994), and as a result, it was quickly stricken from his record.

2) *Eye of the Beholder* (1999): Over the years Ashley Judd has earned a reputation as an actress who can be counted on to appear in a thriller every couple of years or so. In 1999, two years after the mediocre *Kiss the Girls* (1997), she starred in Stephen Elliot's[6] *Eye of the Beholder*, but these release dates are deceptive as the two films were actually filmed around the same time. *Beholder* languished on the shelf for quite a while before it was finally released to theaters, and it is easy to see why. In it, Judd departed from her typical role as the victim/heroine and instead played the tormented black widow-esque killer who spends the film being pursued by an equally unhinged federal agent played by Ewan McGregor. Despite interesting performances from both actors, the film was undone by its painfully pretentious attempts to elevate the material to a higher artistic level. The result is an incomprehensible mishmash that is only kept from being irritating by being so incredibly dull that it becomes impossible to feel anything while watching it.

3) *Cobra* (1986): "Crime is the disease. Meet the cure," read the tag line to this hilariously inept collection of all the worst 1980s action movie clichés. The cure here being Sylvester Stallone's titular hero, the monosyllabic Marion "Cobra" Cobretti, a "shoot first, ask questions later" cop in desperate need of a good shave. When a young Amazonian model

---

6 Whose promising career following the cult success of his *The Adventures of Priscilla, Queen of the Desert* (1994) was effectively ended by the failure of this unfortunate follow-up.

named Ingrid[7] becomes the only person who can identify the vicious serial killer known as the Night Slasher,[8] Cobra and his partner work to protect her and search for the madman before he kills again. This dismal production reunited Stallone with the director of his previous mega-hit *Rambo: First Blood Part II* (1985), George Pan Cosmatos,[9] with a screenplay written by Stallone, based on the book *Fair Game* by Paula Gosling.[10] Stallone would eventually return to the serial killer genre 16 years later with *Eye See You* (2002),[11] which was released directly to video, yet still manages to be the better movie of the two.

4) *The Watcher* **(2000):** Sometimes actors really have to be careful about the promises they make. When Keanu Reeves worked on the unremarkable 1997 production *The Last Time I Committed Suicide*, he was asked by that film's assistant director Joe Charbanic to make a cameo as a serial killer in a production Charbanic was about to direct called *The Watcher*. Reeves agreed and thanks to his name being attached to the project, Charbanic and his producers were

---

7 Stallone's then-wife, the six-foot-tall Brigette Nielson in a not-very-convincing red wig.

8 Career bad guy Brian Thompson, who was chosen largely for his ability to make Stallone look intelligent by default.

9 Whose other credits include the highly enjoyable Canadian man-against-rat movie *Of Unknown Origin* (1983) and the cult-western classic *Tombstone* (1993).

10 Proving that Hollywood will pretty much do anything if it means not having to have an original thought, Gosling's book was filmed once again, nine years later. *Fair Game* (1995) was supposed to be the film that made supermodel Cindy Crawford a movie star, but we all know how that turned out. It costarred Baldwin brother, Billy (the one with the *really* obnoxious smirk, or is that Stephen?) who, like Stallone, spends much of the movie needing a shave.

11 Which was filmed and released in Europe as *D-Tox*.

able to get the film made. Unfortunately for Reeves, his part in the script had been greatly enlarged and was no longer the small cameo he had agreed to. Due to the initial deal he had made with Charbanic, he would only be paid union scale for his participation while his costars James Spader and Marisa Tomei were each going to earn million-dollar paychecks for their roles. Reeves, with some justification, wanted to get out the movie, but he stayed on out of fear of being hit by a lawsuit similar to the one Kim Basinger had lost.[12] He agreed to stay in the movie, but only if his participation was given minimal focus in the film's publicity campaign.[13] The result was one of the worst movies of his career; the film was amateurishly directed and completely lacked suspense or credibility. Luckily, having disassociated himself from the production, it didn't harm his career. James Spader, on the other hand, would soon be forced to find work on television.

5) *Basic Instinct* **(1992):** Okay, I'll admit that I have a certain fondness for this famously overwrought psychosexual thriller, but I feel compelled to include it in this list if only for all of the truly awful direct-to-video rip-offs it has spawned over the years,[14] as well as its connection to screenwriter Joe Eszterhas.[15] But as far as I'm concerned, director

---

12 Basinger had been sued by the producers of *Boxing Helena* for reneging on her verbal promise to star in their movie. The jury sided with the producers and forced Basinger to pay them $9 million in damages. This judgment was later successfully appealed (after Basinger was forced to declare bankruptcy) and the producers eventually agreed to an unnamed settlement from the beleaguered beauty.

13 This didn't stop the producers from putting him on the poster.

14 Those of you who recognize the name Shannon Whirry know exactly what I am talking about.

15 Arguably the least-talented writer to ever earn millions in Hollywood, and that's saying *a lot*.

Beware of frosty blondes bearing ice picks.
(Sharon Stone and Michael Douglas in *Basic Instinct*)

Paul Verhoeven cemented his status as Hollywood's most
pleasingly enigmatic auteur with this film. Like *Total Recall*
(1990), *Showgirls* (1995) and *Starship Troopers* (1997), *Basic
Instinct* is full of enough moments of sly self-consciousness
that it is easy to believe that the film was *meant* to play as a
satire of itself. Good or bad, it is never boring, which is more
than you can say for a lot of films in this genre.

2
The Shape of Things to Come

Halloween

One Halloween night,
a long time ago,
Michael Myers decided that his older sister had to die,
so he killed her with a butcher knife.

He was six years old.

Sent to a hospital for his crime,
Michael was treated by Dr. Sam Loomis,
who at first tried to get through to the catatonic little boy
but stopped when he realized
that what lay beneath those cold black eyes was
purely and simply
evil.

From then on the good doctor dedicated himself to making sure
that Michael never got out into the real world,
but evil can never really be contained
and on the eve of the 15th anniversary of his sister's murder,
Michael escaped from the hospital
and found his way home.

Wearing a mask and stolen work clothes and carrying a knife,
Michael ceased to be Michael and became The Shape
and The Shape was not something that could be stopped.

As the trick or treaters walked the streets and claimed what was
theirs,
The Shape was drawn towards a clever, teenaged babysitter
named Laurie Strode,
who was too old to know that the bogeyman was real
and was far too innocent to ever think
that she would meet him face to face that Halloween night...

The Misfit Genre

No, it's just what's the point? They're all the same. Some stupid killer stalking some big-breasted girl who can't act, who's always running up the stairs when she should be going out the front door. It's insulting.

—Sidney Prescott (Neve Campbell), *Scream* (1996)

It's almost impossible for an adult to understand the appeal of the scary-movie sub-genre known as the slasher flick. During its two major periods of popularity, the early to mid-1980s[1] and the late 1990s, critics and parents have scratched their heads in wonder, unable to figure out why teenagers would be so attracted to these formulaic films whose rules were so relentlessly observed by their filmmakers that they were actually parodied by Wes Craven's *Scream* (1996), the film which inadvertently instigated their second-wave of popularity. What they could not appreciate was the fact that those very rules that made these films so predictable were also precisely what made them resonate so strongly with their young audience.

---

1 Following the success of John Carpenter's *Halloween* (1978) and Sean Cunningham's *Friday the 13th* (1980).

For those of you unfamiliar with these rules, they are:

1) The main characters in a slasher film will all be teenagers or, at the very least, adults who behave like teenagers.[2]

2) The majority of these characters are hedonists who are solely devoted to having a good time. They are usually unnecessarily cruel to each other but reserve most of their viciousness for anyone who is the slightest bit different from them.

3) The exception to rule #2 is the film's main character who is usually a pretty, young woman who refuses to join in with her friends when they drink, do drugs or have sex. She is kind to everyone and concerned about her future, and she makes sure she always gets her work done.

4) Wherever these characters are gathered—a quiet suburb, a summer camp, a school, a vacation retreat, etc.—they are joined by a mysterious figure with a disturbing past who is overcome with a need for revenge. Sometimes he/she/it is young enough to go after the peers who were directly responsible for the horrible incident that disfigured them, humiliated them or resulted in the death of a loved one, but older psychos are happy to go after kids who just *behave* like the original malefactors. Every now and then, the killer has no

---

2 In either case, the cast will almost never be the same age as the characters they are portraying. One of the most extreme cases of this being the lamentable *Slaughter High* (1986), which features scream queen and former Bond Girl Caroline Munro as one of the students. She was 37 when the movie was filmed, beating the record of implausibility set by the 34-year-old Stockyard Channing when she played the part of Rizzo in the hit musical *Grease* (1978).

genuine motive for attacking the kids beyond the fact that they're evil, but that's pretty rare.

5) For many of the murders, the camera takes on the point of view of the killer, especially as he/she/it stalks their prey. As we watch what is happening through the killer's eyes, the sound-track is taken over by a sparse and unnerving musical theme.

6) The killer, who is usually very creative when it comes to how he/she/it kills people, will attack the teenagers as they are engaging in activities they shouldn't.

7) All of the characters are now dead, except for the shy and pretty do-gooder whose unwillingness to succumb to peer pressure has kept her alive. Through her intelligence and ingenuity she is able to: a) find out who the killer is and b) stop them from ever killing again. At least once she will think the killer is dead, only to discover that he/she/it still has some life in them. She then kills them again, only this time she *really* kills them,[3] and we leave her knowing that she has been profoundly and forever changed by this terrifying and har-rowing experience.[4]

While it may be hard to understand why anyone would be so attracted to a genre of film whose rules and archetypes essentially negate any chance of something unpredictable

---

3 That is unless the movie is successful, in which case the killer will be resurrected for the sequel.

4 For a more thorough and academic view of the "Final Girl" cliché, I urge you to take a look at Carol J. Clover's book *Men, Women and Chainsaws: Gender in the Modern Horror Film* (1992). Her views on the subject remain the most insightful I have ever encountered.

happening in the course of the narrative, it is actually the predictability of these films that makes them so appealing. Like the audience that *wants* the story's couple to end up happily together at the end of the romantic comedy (despite the complaints from most critics that such endings are invariably trite and unrealistic), the audience that comes back to watch slasher movies again and again does so because it loves the film's clichés.

What then is the appeal of this formula?

To understand it you have to go back in your memories to that time in your life when you were young. If you were a popular and happy teenager with loads of friends who always knew where the party was and what to do once it started, maybe you'll be a bit bewildered by what you're about to read. If, on the other hand, you were a nerd or a geek or a misfit or an outcast in any sort of way, then you know why the appeal of a good slasher movie is clear. You went to see slasher movies to see the "popular kids" pay for the fun you knew they were having when you were at home playing video games, watching TV with your parents or finishing up your homework. Slasher films appealed to your feelings of being inadequate or insecure about yourself, and let's face it, everyone has felt this way at one time or another.

At the height of the slasher movie boom, there was a lot of talk about how these films were dangerous because of how they allowed the audience to identify with the killer as he/she/it slaughtered their victims. What these concerned critics failed to recognize was just who the victims in these movies were.

They were jerks.

The kids who were killed in these movies were people who exhibited the most boorish kinds of behavior. They were rude, selfish, violent, proudly ignorant and obsessed with their own gratification. Often they themselves were responsible for the incident that had driven the movie's maniac to pursue the cathartic power of mutilation in the first place.

The truth was that most of these movies weren't very frightening because most of the characters were deliberately one-dimensional. If there were scares in a slasher movie, they were of the quick gross-out variety, which were generally too over-the-top to be real.

More importantly, these formulaic films allow their audiences the chance to feel good about itself. They don't identify with the jerks being killed, but with the heroine, the sweet pretty girl who the jerks made fun of. It is imperative that she survives and ultimately kills the psycho because she represents the audience. For the first three-quarters of the film, the audience roots for the killer because he/she/it is ridding the world of a lot of people who only made the planet a more miserable place to be, but as soon as the killer starts pursuing the heroine, the audience's allegiance shifts. Recognizing her as a good and decent person, the audience sides with this last survivor because they see themselves in her. Her triumph over the maniac is a victory for decency, nonconformity and for the audience's own social inadequacies.

Kids loved these films, not for their unquenchable thirst for graphic violence (well, okay, that might have been the reason *some* kids liked them, but I honestly think they were the minority), but because these movies made them feel good about the fact that they didn't fit in at school. Much has been made about the extreme morality of these films—where sex and partying is considered a capital offense—but most of the kids watching understood that the true crime being committed by these doomed teenagers was the squandering of their futures for the quick fix of immediate pleasure. This message served as a balm for every kid who was mocked and laughed at by his or her more popular peers.

In reality, teenage angst takes a lot of time to heal—years in fact—but a good slasher movie provides a cathartic effect in 90 minutes or less, and that is the reason for their popularity. I imagine that as the next generation comes of age these films will once again play an important part in the scary movie landscape. Like its psychotic antagonists, just when we think the slasher movie is really dead, it's going to jump right back at us, knowing that as long as there are dissatisfied and unhappy teenagers out there, it can never die.

How It Happened

Irwin Yablans' idea was simple. He wanted to make a horror movie about baby-sitters. Sexy, teenage baby-sitters. Wanting the movie to be cheap to produce and easy to film, he decided that its story should take place over the course of a single day, but which one? The choice seemed obvious. October 31—the day celebrated throughout North America as Halloween—had long ago been designated the spookiest day of the year. With this in mind he did some research and made a startling discovery. Over the course of the 70 odd years that films had been made, not a single feature had been named *Halloween* or even had the name of the holiday as a part of its title. This seemed like a good omen, and he started looking for a filmmaker who could take this simple concept and give it life.

At that time a 29-year-old director named John Carpenter was making a name for himself with his first two low-budget movies. The first was a comedy takeoff of Stanley Kubrick's *2001: A Space Odyssey* (1968) entitled *Dark Star* (1974) that had started out as his student film but was eventually released to theaters, where it earned a cult reputation on the midnight movie circuit. He followed up *Dark Star* with a modern update of the classic Howard Hawks western *Rio Bravo* (1959), called *Assault on Precinct 13* (1976) that went ignored in North America but was a big hit overseas.[5] Impressed by what Carpenter seemed able to do with such low budgets, Yablans asked him if he was interested in making *Halloween*. Carpenter told him he was and surprised Yablans by telling him that he could make the film in four weeks for $300,000, which, even in the 1970s, was a very low budget. Yablans agreed to pay the filmmaker $10,000 and 10% of the film's net profits.[6]

In order to get financing for the film, Yablans turned to a Syrian film producer and director named Moustapha Akkad,[7] who at the time was working on his epic *Lion of the Desert* (1980). He gave them the $300,000 after meeting with Yablans and Carpenter in London, although he wondered how it would be possible to make a good film for so little money.

---

5 A remake of *Precinct 13* was released in 2005 to mixed reviews and a mediocre box office.

6 At the time, Carpenter—reasonably—assumed that he would never see a dime from this part of their agreement, but it eventually made him a lot more money than he ever could have dreamed of.

7 Beyond his role as the man behind the *Halloween* film franchise, Akkad is best known as the director and producer of *The Message,* aka *Mohammed, Messenger of God,* (1976), an epic about the life of the Prophet of Islam in which—in accordance with Islamic law—Mohammed and his family—with the exception of his uncle Hamza, played by Anthony Quinn—never appear on-screen.

When it came time to write the script, Carpenter decided he didn't know enough to characterize the film's young female protagonists properly, so he asked his friend Debra Hill, who had worked as the script supervisor on *Assault On Precinct 13*, to co-write and produce the film with him. Both of them were huge fans of Alfred Hitchcock and looked to his classic *Psycho* as their inspiration.[8] But unlike *Psycho*, whose antagonist Norman Bates was a completely human monster, their villain would be something else. Though their script would make it clear that Michael Myers[9] was a man and not some kind of vampire or zombie, it would also suggest that he was compelled to commit his murders by a force beyond the realm of normal humanity.

Even though *Halloween* and *Friday the 13th* are the films most often credited as the parents that gave birth to the slasher movie genre, some have argued that its true originator was Bob Clark's *Black Christmas*, a Canadian film made four years before *Halloween* in 1974. In interviews, Clark—who today is best known as the director of that perennial holiday classic *A Christmas Story* (1983)—has suggested that it was he and not Yablans who put the idea for *Halloween* into John Carpenter's head. According to Clark, Carpenter was a big fan of *Black Christmas* and once asked him if he ever planned to make a sequel to it. Clark claims he told Carpenter that he had no plans to ever make a sequel, but that if he did, then he would have the film take place a year later, after the first film's killer has escaped from a mental hospital and goes back to the campus where the first film took place. The difference would be that instead of taking place during Christmas, the sequel would take place during Halloween, which would be reflected in the film's title. Carpenter has apparently denied Clark's version of events.

Knowing that their budget would not allow them to hire seasoned professionals, Carpenter and Hill looked to their friends to fill out their crew. The most professional member of their team was their cinematographer, Dean Cundey, who had already shot 11 features[10] before he made *Halloween*. Tommy Lee Wallace[11] was hired as the production designer and his then-wife, Nancy Loomis, was given the part of the acerbic Annie. Nick Castle,[12] a friend of Carpenter's from his days at the University of Southern California, asked if he could just hang around the set and observe what was going on. Carpenter told him that if he was going to be there all day, then he might as well have something to do and cast him as The Shape.

Having seen her performance in Brian De Palma's *Carrie* (1977), Carpenter wrote the role of Linda specifically for the young actress P.J. Soles, but—assuming she wouldn't take the part—he went looking for a similar kind of actress to play the mischievous blonde. His efforts proved unwarranted when Soles showed up to the audition for him and made it clear that she would be happy to appear in his

---

8 Even going so far as to name one of the characters Sam Loomis after the part John Gavin played in Hitchcock's classic.

9 Carpenter—in a slightly twisted homage—named the character after the very kind man who had distributed *Assault On Precinct 13*.

10 Including the last film in the infamous Ilsa series, *Ilsa, Harem Keeper of the Oil Sheiks* (1976), and the easy-to-forget camp horror movie *Satan's Cheerleaders* (1977).

11 Who would eventually direct the third—and most controversial—film in the *Halloween* series and who is best known as the director of the popular Stephen King television mini-series *It* (1990).

12 Another future director, Castle—the son of a popular Hollywood choreographer—has specialized in making children's films since he appeared in *Halloween*, the most famous of which are *The Last Starfighter* (1984) and *Dennis the Menace* (1993). But his best film is easily the classic 1986 fantasy tearjerker *The Boy Who Could Fly*.

film.[13] Soles also tried to get her then-husband Dennis Quaid the role of Bob, Linda's boyfriend, but he had already been cast in *Are You In the House Alone?* (1978), a made-for-TV horror movie. The role went instead to John Michael Graham, a first-time film actor who never made another movie after *Halloween*.

As it turned out, the most difficult roles to cast were the film's two leads, Laurie Strode and Dr. Loomis. For the part of Laurie, Carpenter wanted to cast an actress named Anne Lockhart (the daughter of June Lockhart, who played moms on both *Lassie* and *Lost in Space*), but she had just been cast in a new TV series called *Battlestar Galactica* and decided that she didn't want to star in a low-budget horror movie.[14]

The second actress to get his attention was also the daughter of a famous mother, but she also had a very famous father as well. Jamie Lee Curtis was the oldest daughter of

"Who was the killer in *Halloween*?" Michael Myers, right? Wrong. Check the credits. The masked maniac in *Halloween* is credited as The Shape. Wanting to give the character an aura of supernatural invulnerability, Carpenter and Hill made a clear distinction between Michael Myers, the man, and The Shape. This is further borne out by their decision to cast two different actors to play the adult killer. Nick Castle plays the character whenever he wears the mask, but for the one shot at the end where Michael's face has been revealed, he is played by an actor named Tony Moran. There were two reasons for this. The first was to implicitly suggest that Michael was not Michael when he wore the mask and the second was because Carpenter and Hill wanted the unmasked killer to look like a normal—almost angelic—young man and not the vicious killer he really was.

Tony Curtis and Janet Leigh. She had very little acting experience when she auditioned for the part of Laurie, having only appeared for one season on the short-lived 1977 sitcom version of the Cary Grant comedy *Operation Petticoat* (1959). Both Hill and Carpenter were intrigued by Curtis because she was a fresh and new talent, but also because she was the daughter of *Psycho*'s Marion Crane. Casting her would most likely give their small film some publicity it might otherwise never receive, and for this second reason she got the job.

In the end, finding a Laurie proved a lot easier than finding the right Dr. Loomis. Carpenter so desperately wanted a name actor in the role that he set aside $25,000 out of the film's tiny budget to get one, but it was still an insignificant amount of money and not nearly enough to get many actors to appear in a grubby little horror movie. The first actor to reject the part was Peter Cushing, an English actor who had many loyal fans thanks to his appearances as Baron Von Frankenstein and Dr. Van Helsing in a series of popular movies made by the British Hammer Studios. He had just appeared in the massively successful *Star Wars* (1977) the year before and he had no interest in a tiny little project like *Halloween*. Carpenter and Hill then turned to Cushing's frequent adversary in the Hammer films, Christopher Lee, who

---

13 After appearing in *Carrie, Halloween* and the infamous John Travolta TV movie *The Boy in the Plastic Bubble* (1976), P.J. Soles had already earned herself a spot in the cult movie hall of fame, but she earned a special place of honor in the pantheon when—a year after appearing in *Halloween*—she took the role of Riff Randell in Alan Arkush's beloved comedy tribute to The Ramones, *Rock and Roll High School* (1979).

14 After her show was canceled, Lockhart changed her mind about low-budget horror movies and appeared in several of them, including taking a cameo as a younger version of a character played by her mother June in the infamously campy John Carl Buechler movie *Troll* (1986), a film which also includes performances by *Law & Order*'s Michael Moriarty, Sonny Bono, *WKRP in Cincinnati's* Gary Sandy) and *Seinfeld's* Julia Louis Dreyfus.

had essentially reinvented the part of Count Dracula in the 1950s and 1960s. He too wasn't interested, though years later he would admit to Hill that not taking the part was the greatest mistake of his career.[15] As Carpenter and Hill were

Having since established herself as both a talented comedic and dramatic actress, it's easy to forget that for a time early in her career, Jamie Lee Curtis was often referred to as The Scream Queen. She earned the nickname due to the fact that she starred in a long run of low-budget horror movies following the success of *Halloween*. The first was *The Fog* (1980), John Carpenter's first feature film after *Halloween*, which also costarred her mother. After that came *Prom Night* (1980), *Terror Train* (1980), *Roadgames* (1981) and the inevitable *Halloween II* (1981). The term Scream Queen is now commonly used to refer to any actress who has earned a reputation among cult movie fans (they even have a magazine devoted to them called *Femme Fatale*), but Curtis' career after these films has been so successful that people forget she was one of the very first. This despite the fact that she has returned to the genre several times since then in films such as *Mother's Boys* (1994), *Halloween: H20* (1998), *Virus* (1999) and a cameo at the beginning of *Halloween: Resurrection* (2002). Given the often negative feelings people have about these scary movies, Curtis has stated in interviews that she finds it ironic that the roles she played in those early, low-budget genre films were a lot less demeaning and more artistically demanding than roles she played in more mainstream Hollywood movies. Back when she was a Scream Queen she played intelligent and resourceful young women who were often the only ones who had what it took to save the day. As proof of her point—she wasn't required to do an unnecessary nude scene in a film until she played a hooker in her first big budget studio comedy, John Landis' *Trading Places* (1983).

busy looking for older horror movie icons, it was Yablans who suggested that they consider the British character actor Donald Pleasance. Pleasance had appeared in several horror movies throughout his career, but he was best remembered by movie fans as the blind forger in the classic WWII adventure film *The Great Escape* (1963), so it seemed like an inspired suggestion. Assuming that he would reject it as everyone else had, they offered the role to him and much to their surprise he accepted, although their offer of $25,000 would only secure his services for a week.

Later, just before they started filming his scenes, Pleasance admitted to Carpenter that he didn't really understand the character or the script and that the only reason he took the role was because his daughter—who was a musician—really liked the score Carpenter had written for his movie *Assault On Precinct 13*. Taking her word that Carpenter had to be talented to come up with an innovative soundtrack like that, Pleasance decided to take a gamble and appear in the little film. On the set his initial leeriness turned into enthusiasm when he saw how hard everyone involved in the production was willing to work, and for the week that he worked, he refused to behave like a prima donna and joined in whenever help was needed to move boxes or pull cable.[16]

---

15 Though it could be said that he made up for it a few decades later when he played the parts of villains in the two biggest movie franchises in recent memory, playing Count Dooku in *Star Wars: Attack of the Clones* (2002) and the evil wizard Saruman in the first two *Lord of the Rings* films.

16 Ironically, it would be Pleasance—who was initially reluctant to appear in the film—who would become the actor most associated with the *Halloween* franchise. Once asked if he would ever stop appearing in the *Halloween* franchise, Pleasance answered that he would draw the line at starring in *Halloween 22*, but would keep on playing Dr. Loomis until then. Unfortunately his death from complications following heart surgery in 1995 kept him from making this happen.

The film was shot in Hollywood with some exterior shots filmed in South Pasadena. The crew did a good job disguising a Los Angeles neighborhood as a small town in Illinois. In order to get the proper sense of autumn that the film's title date required, the crew carried around boxes of dried leaves that were blown across the streets during filming before being hurriedly raked up and reboxed for the next day's scenes.

Despite the movie's low budget and tight schedule, Carpenter was emboldened by new technology to try something virtually unheard of in non-studio films at that time. As a big fan of Orson Welles' legendary long tracking shot at the beginning of *Touch of Evil* (1958), Carpenter wanted to open his film with a long, uninterrupted shot, filmed from the perspective of young Michael Myers. It would have been impossible for a limited production such as *Halloween* to accomplish this even a few months earlier, but thanks to the invention of the Steadicam—a device that allowed for steady and fluid movement of the camera without the use of cumbersome dolly tracks—Carpenter was able to get the shot he wanted in a single night of filming. Not only was this shot extremely innovative for its time, but it would later be copied in virtually every slasher movie that followed.

Also to be copied was the film's unnerving, minimalist score, which was composed in two days by Carpenter himself. Working on his synthesizer, Carpenter remembered back to when his father had bought him a bongo drum and taught him how to play it in $5/4$ time and replicated that sound as the film's theme. His work as a composer proved as effective as his work as a director. One studio executive who saw the film without its score told Carpenter that she didn't think it was scary, but she later changed her mind when she saw it with the full soundtrack. Irwin Yablans also saw the effect the film's score had on audiences when he noticed during a screening that some audience members weren't covering their eyes during the scary parts, but instead covering their ears.

To this day, John Carpenter has claimed that making *Halloween* was the best time he ever had in his professional life, but when it was all over, he never could have expected how influential and important his little horror movie would eventually become.

The Aftermath

None of the major studios were willing to even touch *Halloween*, which they saw as an unpleasant little film that no one in their right mind would want to see. So Irwin Yablans and his business partner Joseph Wolf decided that they would distribute it to theaters themselves. Through their contacts and some hard work, they got the film into a handful of theaters around the country. They had almost no money at all to promote the film, so how the film did in these first few locations would help determine how much more time and effort they would put in to promoting the film. Box office receipts were average the first night, but got better the second night and then even better on the third. Yablans and Wolf quickly realized that what they had on their hands was a true word-of-mouth hit, a film that people told all of their friends that they had to see. This success allowed them to get the movie into more theaters and spend some money on advertising. Critics began to notice the film, and their reaction—for the most part—was enthusiastically positive.[17] The film would go on to become the most successful mainstream independently released film of all time, earning $70 million at the box office.[18]

Halloween's success was a revelation to film producers and studio executives who were stunned and excited by the prospect of making $70 million out of a $300,000 investment. One of these individuals was a man named Sean S. Cunningham who was best known at the time as the producer of Wes Craven's *The Last House On the Left* (1972), one of the most controversial horror movies of the 1970s. Having just produced and directed two family films[19] that failed to make any money, he decided that his next project should be a guaranteed hit and he looked to *Halloween* as his inspiration.

Looking around for a date as ominous as October 31 to center his film around, he settled on Friday the 13th, a day commonly associated by the superstitious as being unlucky. Having no idea what the film would be about, he took out an ad in *Variety* announcing that he was beginning work on *Friday the 13th*. Thanks to the success of *Halloween*, he instantly found financing for his film and went to work on making it. When the film was in the can, the same studios that had been unwilling to distribute *Halloween* were eager to

---

17 Roger Ebert gave the film four stars—his highest rating—and compared it to *Psycho*. Interestingly, he spent much of his review defending the film's violence, which is odd since there is actually very little serious violence in the movie, especially when compared to similar kinds of films. He would later denounce slasher films on his TV show for being a menace to society.

18 Its record would later go on to be broken by *The Blair Witch Project* (1999), *My Big Fat Greek Wedding* (2002) and *The Passion of the Christ* (2004). No mainstream film, though, has come even close to being as successful as the most profitable independent film of all time, Gerard Damiano's infamous *Deep Throat* (1972).

19 Both of which were inspired directly by the success of Michael Ritchie's *The Bad News Bears* (1978).

get their hands on Cunningham's inferior film. Paramount Studios ended up with the film and it was so profitable that they ended up making seven sequels to it before they finally sold the rights to the franchise to another company.

As the first *Halloween* rip-off to turn a serious profit, *Friday the 13th* was the film that opened the floodgates and caused a wave of cheap slasher films to be made over the next decade. Unfortunately, none of these films came close to being as good as *Halloween* and most managed to be even worse than *Friday the 13th*.

Among these inferior clones, one has to include *Halloween*'s sequels, none of which have come close to equaling the original. *Halloween II* was written by Carpenter and Hill, but they have since acknowledged that they made the serious error of setting it immediately after the events of the first film, meaning that its heroine—a returning Jamie Lee Curtis—spends most of the film unconscious in a hospital bed. The film's biggest revelation was that Laurie Strode had been adopted and was actually Laurie Myers, Michael's little sister, which explained why he had been drawn to her in the original. For the third film, Carpenter and Hill decided to

After the success of *Halloween* and *Friday the 13th*, many filmmakers looked to other days of the week and holidays with which they could set their films. Their work produced, among others, *Mother's Day* (1980), *Prom Night* (1980), *Home Sweet Home* (1980), which takes place on Thanksgiving, *Christmas Evil* (1980), *To All A Goodnight* (1980), *New Year's Evil* (1981), *My Bloody Valentine* (1981), *Graduation Day* (1981), *Silent Night, Deadly Night* (1984) and *April Fool's Day* (1986).

make a movie that had nothing to do with the first two in the series. The result was *Halloween III: Season of the Witch* (1982), which told the tale of a madman who planned to murder children around the world by selling magically lethal Halloween masks. The flawed but still entertaining film was angrily rejected by fans who had wanted to see another movie about Michael Myers. That film's failure seemed to signal the end of the series, but then in 1988 there came *Halloween 4:The Return of Michael Myers*, which was then followed by *Halloween 5: The Revenge of Michael Myers* (1989) and then *Halloween: The Curse of Michael Myers* (1995). All of these films were pale copies of the original, and the last one was so bad that it looked like the series was finally done, but then three years later someone had another bright idea.

The 20th anniversary of the first film was fast approaching and the people at Dimension Films realized that it would be really cool if John Carpenter and Jamie Lee Curtis got back together and made the next film in the series—one in which the events of the last three films would be ignored in favor of a continuation with the first two films in the series. Curtis was intrigued by the idea and agreed to do it, but Carpenter had decided that he was no longer interested in the characters he had created and turned the project down. *Halloween: H2O*—as the film was eventually called—was directed by Steve Miner, who had previously worked on a couple of films in the *Friday the 13th* series. The result was the franchise's best sequel, but it still failed to match the tension and terror of the original. Curtis played Laurie Strode one last time in 2002, when she made a cameo at the beginning of *Halloween: Resurrection*. Directed by Rick

Rosenthal—who had also made *Halloween II*[20]—this last film managed to squander all that was good about *H20* and the result is one of the worst films in the series.

Also Look For

If you're interested in *Halloween*, your best bet is to find Anchor Bay Entertainment's 25th Anniversary Edition, a two-disc set that includes a commentary by John Carpenter, Debra Hill and Jamie Lee Curtis, as well as an 87-minute documentary about the film entitled *Halloween—A Cut Above the Rest*. Also of interest is a previous 1999 limited edition that includes the film, as well as the television edit of the film that contains scenes that do not appear in the original. It's out of print, but copies can still be found online if you look for them.

---

20 And who had previously taken an Alan Smithee credit for his work on the abysmal made-for-cable sequel to Alfred Hitchcock's classic *The Birds* (1963), *The Birds II: Land's End* (1994). Alan Smithee is the name that filmmakers were allowed to use when they could prove that interference from a film's producers or studio resulted in a movie so bad that having their name attached to it could negatively impact their career.

The Fine Art of the Hack and Slash

The Good

Halloween may be the best slasher movie of all time, but there are several others that manage to transcend the clichés of the genre and are worth checking out.

1) *Scream* **(1996):** Sometimes the most revolutionary ideas in film are also the simplest. In 1995, a struggling actor named Kevin Williamson had an idea that—for better or worse—briefly changed how horror movies were made in Hollywood until a backlash against his innovations changed the paradigm once again. But it had not been his intention to inspire a mini-revolution in the genre when he came up with his brilliant idea; he just wanted to make some quick cash. Low on funds, Williamson had decided to write a horror movie script on the slim chance that he could sell it to some B-movie producer for the straight-to-video market. What happened with Scream is one of those minor miracles that keep people coming to Hollywood year after year, hoping that it might happen to them.

Williamson wanted to bring something different to his screenplay, something that would make it unique. Like all horror movie fans, Williamson had always been annoyed when lazy screenwriters forced their characters to do things that defied all notions of common sense. Why, for example, did people in horror movies always split up when it would be much safer for them to stay together? Why would characters stop and have sex when their lives were in danger? Why hide in a closet when a person could have easily gone out the open door or window? Williamson wanted to tackle these clichés head on with his script. He decided that his characters would be as familiar with all of the old horror movie clichés as he was, which added a new perspective to the dialogue and action. Whenever the characters were faced with one of these clichés, they had two choices—embrace it or reject it—but what made Williamson's script so thrilling was that both choices could easily lead to death.

Like *An American Werewolf in London* (1981), the screenplay he wrote worked as both horror and comedy. The film

"Do you like scary movies, Sidney?"
(Neve Campbell and Rose McGowan in *Scream*)

was a smart satire of the dumbest of all the horror sub-genres, the slasher film. What he added to the mix was the witty postmodern self-reflection, which had not yet been explored in the horror genre. Each moment in the film worked on two levels: on the first, the film's plot followed the established format of the slasher genre, and then on another level, these same rules were being acknowledged and mocked by both the filmmakers and the characters in the story. A constant barrage of pop culture references was added, which the audience could easily recognize but at the same time made the story seem more artificial and deliberate. The whole screenplay worked as both an epic in-joke for fans of the genre and as a gripping thriller for uninitiated newcomers.

He called his script Scary Movie, and it proved to be such a great read that several studios tried to get their hands on it. It ended up being bought by Dimension Films, a niche studio created by Miramax's Bob and Harvey Weinstein solely to release low-budget genre films. It was Bob Weinstein who got the script into the hands of horror movie legend Wes Craven. Just three years earlier Craven had made a similar kind of film with *New Nightmare* (1993), which had reunited him with Freddy Krueger, his most famous creation. Craven agreed to make the film and assembled a cast full of the hottest young stars Hollywood had to offer. Television star Neve Campbell was hired to play the lead and Skeet Ulrich[1] was given his first major role as her boyfriend. Drew Barrymore agreed to make a cameo in the film in the role of Casey, whose early death in the film was a deliberate nod to

---

1 An actor who bore a very strong resemblance to another star Craven had discovered years earlier, Johnny Depp.

Janet Leigh in *Psycho*. Courtney Cox, now a major star thanks to her role on the sitcom *Friends*, was cast as Gale Weathers, an unlikable but resourceful reporter.

The film, retitled *Scream*, was released during the Christmas season of 1996. Attendance started out slowly at the box office, but its earnings kept improving week after week. Word of mouth kept it in theaters where it eventually became a major hit. A sequel was rushed into production and released the following year. It wasn't as good, but it was still a lot of fun to watch. In 2000, a final sequel was released and by this time enthusiasm for the series was beginning to fade. For fans of horror movies, *Scream* represented both a blessing and curse. Hollywood once again became aware of how profitable these kinds of movies could be, and started releasing them at a record pace. Unfortunately too many producers overlooked the fact that *Scream*'s success was the result of a clever screenplay, and instead decided that what the kids wanted to see was hot, young actors get killed in fun, new ways. Instead of attempting something unique, like *Scream* had done, the new films were simply content to copy the *Scream* formula with less rewarding results. And while most of these films made some attempt to echo *Scream*'s humor, the joke had—by that point—grown thin.[2]

Williamson moved on to create the TV show *Dawson's Creek*, as well as write screenplays for *The Faculty* (1998) and *Cursed* (2004), but as of this writing, he has yet to replicate the achievement of his first screenplay. Today fans look upon

---

2 This was proven in 2000 with the release of *Scary Movie*, a comic parody of *Scream* and its many imitators, which was also produced by Dimension Films. The fact that *Scary Movie*'s filmmakers felt comfortable satirizing a movie that itself had been a satire illustrates how constant imitation has greatly dulled *Scream*'s initial achievements.

the film *Scream* with a mixture of wariness and affection. Blaming the film for the detritus that followed, some people insist *Scream* was never as good as people initially thought it was. Its influence might have faded quickly, but when you go back and watch it again, you can easily see that the film itself still burns bright.

2) *Sleepaway Camp* (1983): Badly directed, acted and written, this low-budget effort redeems itself with one of the most memorable endings and final shots in the history of scary movies. Also worthy of note is the odd performance by Desiree Gould as the (very!) eccentric Aunt Martha. In the beginning, her unique acting choices appeared completely out of place in a movie like this, but when the final twist is revealed, she became a truly unnerving character. It was followed by two very bad sequels that bear no resemblance to the original, but have the odd distinction of starring Bruce Springsteen's younger sister Pamela as the crazy transsexual killer.

3) *Urban Legend* (1998): The best of the many movies that were released after the success of the first *Scream*, it works mostly because of a clever concept that has the killer committing murders based on famous urban legends.[3] Like *Scream*, it is smart enough to acknowledge its clichés as it follows them, and it has a lot of fun taking jibes at its own cast with references to *Dawson's Creek* and costar Rebecca

---

3 Which, as an author of a book entitled *Urban Legends*, is a twist on the genre I can readily appreciate. And I'm not afraid to admit that this footnote amounts to little more than a cheap plug for my previous work. It's still available in stores and online.

Gayheart's work in a famous Noxema skin-care commercial. Avoid the sequel *Urban Legend: Final Cut* (2000). Not only is it boring, it doesn't even keep up the urban legends gimmick established in the first film.

4) *Jason X* (*Friday the 13th Part 10*) (2001): The best installment (although I also really like part 6, *Jason Lives*) in the most popular slasher movie series of all time, *Jason X* takes

The world's most dangerous mama's boy.
(Jason Voorhees in one of *Friday the 13th* sequels)

the famous goalie-mask-wearing maniac and drops him into the future where he can just as easily kill pot-smoking vixens in virtual reality as he can in real life. Thanks to a funny script, good performances by the mostly Canadian cast and some great special effects, this is a more entertaining film than the much more successful *Freddy Vs. Jason* (2003).

5) The Stepfather (1987): This film resembles the style of serial killer movies that would follow in the 1990s. The film rises above the ordinary, thanks to an amazing performance by character actor Terry O'Quinn—best known for his performances on the TV shows *Alias* and *Lost*—as Jerry Blake, the title character, a man who has killed many times in his quest to find the perfect family. Two sequels followed, but neither of them are worth looking for.

The Not-So-Good

To be honest, most slasher movies are pretty awful, but these five films can definitely be found floating at the bottom of the barrel.

1) *Cheerleader Camp* **(1987):** Despite featuring an amazing B-movie cast filled with a balding former pop star (Leif Garrett), a former female Ninja (Lucinda Dickey from *Ninja III: The Domination*, 1984), a bad-teen-movie goddess (Betsy Russell from *Private School*, 1983) and two former *Playboy*

---

4 Who later became infamous as only the second centerfold in the magazine's history to become an adult video star.

playmates, (Rebecca Ferratti and Teri Weigel,)[4] this attempt to combine horror with comedy manages to be neither scary nor funny. Released as *Bloody Pom-Poms* in Europe, it may not be the worst slasher movie of all time, but it is easily the most disappointing. Incredibly, a sequel was made, but was released as an unrelated film entitled *The Millennium Countdown* (1991).

2) *The Burning* (1981): Wasting even more potential than *Cheerleader Camp*, *The Burning* features a future Oscar winner (Holly Hunter), a future Tony winner and Emmy nominee (*Seinfeld*'s Jason Alexander) and the biggest geek to ever date Michelle Pfeiffer (Fisher Stevens). Not only that, but it was also co-written and produced by those future Oscar juggernauts, Miramax's Bob and Harvey Weinstein. The most amazing thing about the film isn't how bad it is but how there isn't even the slightest hint that anybody involved in the production would ever work again, much less achieve greatness.[5] The fact that someone who was in this movie not only met Michelle Pfeiffer, but dated her as well, is enough to boggle anyone's mind.

3) *Sleepaway Camp IV: The Survivor* (Never Completed): This third film in the *Sleepaway Camp* series was canceled after just a few days of filming. Why then am I putting it on the list? Because for years, obsessive fans have actually paid money for bootleg copies of the unedited footage that was

---

5 That's not to say the film doesn't have its defenders. Quentin Tarantino, a director famed for his love of low-budget genre films, has said in an interview that he considers *The Burning* one of the best slasher movies ever made. Personally, I have to admit that I think his defense of *The Burning* is more than a little odd.

shot, and because in 2002, the footage was released on DVD as a fourth disc in a special-limited edition of *Sleepaway Camp* from by Anchor Bay Entertainment. As boring as it is to watch raw unedited footage of *The Survivor*, the footage is so obviously awful that it becomes immediately apparent why the film wasn't finished.

4) *Slumber Party Massacre* **(1982):** Truthfully, there are a lot of films worse than this one that I could put on the list, but I'm including it as an example of equal opportunity awfulness. Directed by Amy Jones and written by Rita Mae Brown, this film proves that women are just as capable of producing violent movies featuring gratuitous scenes of female nudity as men are. A sequel followed in 1987, and it too was written and directed by a woman, Deborah Brock.

5) *I Still Know What You Did Last Summer* **(1998):** Saddled with one of the worst sequel titles ever, this continuation of the drama first introduced in the previous year's *I Know What You Did Last Summer* makes the list because it had a decent budget, some big-name teen stars and a lot of publicity, but still ended up being as bad as most of the home-movie quality direct-to-video projects that glutted the market 15 years earlier.

3
Tragically Delicious

An American Werewolf in London

David and Jack are two young college kids
who are spending their summer backpacking through Europe.

As Jack dreams aloud of romancing beautiful Italian girls in Rome,
he and his friend find themselves stranded in the lonely moors of
Northern England.

They try to claim a respite from the cold and the gloom
by stepping into The Slaughtered Lamb,
a small pub full of unfriendly locals,
who quickly scare them away
but not before warning them
to beware the moon and to stay on the road.

The two young men ignore this advice and soon get very, very lost.

Around them they hear the sound of an animal in their midst.
It is a wolf and it attacks them.

Jack is killed,
but David survives when the beast is shot
by a group of locals from The Slaughtered Lamb.

As the wounded David turns his head
he sees a man where the wolf's body should be,
but before he can say anything about this odd sight
he loses consciousness and finds himself lost in a three-week-long
dream.

He wakes up in a London hospital,
where he is visited by his dead and slowly decomposing friend.

Jack has a message for him.

The full moon is coming
and innocent people are going to die...

Dark Humor

You see, American Werewolf in London *is not a comedy. It's called a comedy. They keep calling it a comedy. It's very funny, I hope. It's* not *a comedy.*

—John Landis, "An Interview with John Landis"

Before John Landis' *An American Werewolf in London* (1981), it was virtually unheard of to combine genuinely funny comedy with serious horror. Abbott and Costello may have met Frankenstein and "The Killer" Boris Karloff,[1] and Gene Wilder may have sung and danced with *Young Frankenstein*[2] (1974), but these films were spoofs that were never intended to really scare anyone. Studio executives didn't want to risk confusing their audiences and they balked at the idea that something could be both funny *and* scary. They weren't the only ones. Critics too were wary of films that tried to combine the disparate sensibilities of seemingly antithetical genres, as evidenced by their initial reaction to Landis' film. They complained that the film didn't seem to know what it wanted to be, but their reaction had more to do with the fact that they were seeing something completely new, rather than with any confusion the film may have had about its own identity.

---

1 In the rather obviously titled films *Abbott and Costello Meet Frankenstein* (1948) and *Abbott and Costello Meet the Killer, Boris Karloff* (1949). They also met the Invisible Man in 1951 and both Dr. Jekyll and Mr. Hyde in 1953.

2 A film whose style was largely inspired by the films of James Whale, whose *Bride of Frankenstein* (1935) was itself something of a spoof of a genre still in its infancy at the time.

An American Werewolf in London knew exactly what it was. It just happened to be the first of its kind.

Its sensibilities were completely defined by John Landis, a young, hyperactive man who loved to make people laugh, but who also wanted to make a movie that was truly and uncompromisingly frightening. The story it tells is tragic—a young man with his whole life ahead of him becomes cursed with a "disease" that causes the deaths of other innocent people, and in the end he has to die. He was merely an unwitting pawn in events he could not control. In a story filled with so much terror and pathos, it is a hallmark to the talents of everyone involved in the production that viewers are able to laugh at all.

While some might point to a film such as George Romero's *Dawn of the Dead* (1978) as a slightly earlier example of combining humor with terror, what they fail to see is that the humor in *An American Werewolf* is not meant to be satiric, as it is in Romero's zombie movie. There are no real jokes or laughs[3] in *Dawn of the Dead*.[4] Instead we are meant to be amused by the fact that mindless zombies, like the mindless living, are attracted to shopping malls. In *An American Werewolf,* the humor comes out of its characters' dialogue and it's actually funny.

The film's humor makes the story more human and as a result we are able empathize with the characters in a way that's impossible in Romero's film.[5] As a viewer, I have heard

---

3 Apart from the one good gag where the zombie gets part of its head taken off by a helicopter blade. It's funnier than it sounds.

4 I have never been able to sit all the way through this film, leading me to personally feel that its reputation in the horror community is wildly overinflated.

5 Whose chief flaw is that its living characters are no more interesting than its dead ones.

dozens of speeches from the tortured undead in films explaining how horrible it is to be cursed, but none has ever come close to feeling so real and perfect than the one-line summation Jack delivers to his friend David. "Have you ever tried talking to a corpse? It's boring!" This is a complaint we can laugh and sympathize with, and it helps us understand why Jack is so adamant about David killing himself. His spirit will only be freed from the limbo once the werewolf's bloodline has ended. Imagine eternity at the world's most boring cocktail party and the idea of a flaming Hell full of sin-punishing demons feels almost joyous in comparison.

The humor also works because it is in such direct contrast with the horror, which still remains extremely brutal to watch. When we see Jack get killed by the werewolf, it is a bloody, horrible mess and his screams are very real cries of pain and terror. It bears no resemblance to the neat and bloodless murders seen so frequently in other similar movies. We can identify with his pain.

This willingness to pursue verisimilitude is most evident in the famous scene in which David Naughton's character transforms into a werewolf for the first time. At the time, this scene was a technical landmark in film, comparable to *King Kong*'s (1933) Empire State Building rampage and *Jurassic Park*'s (1993) computer-generated dinosaurs. For the first time, viewers saw someone transform into a monster before their very eyes without awkward dissolves or cutaways. The special effects were so amazing that a new Academy Award category was added just so it could be honored. But what makes the scene truly memorable today is the way it makes explicit the idea of how incredibly painful such a transformation would really be. It hurts just to look at it. Previous werewolf films glossed over this seemingly major detail, but *An American Werewolf* uses it to add serious insult to David's injury. Not only is he forced to transform into a murderous hellbeast every time the full moon rises, but he also has to suffer the worst pain imaginable to do it.

The impact the film had on the genre wasn't immediate. In the years following its release, horror films—for the most part—continued to err on the side of drama. They may have inserted the occasional joke here and there into their script, but they seldom attempted to combine the two genres the same way *An American Werewolf* did. In 1987, six years after the success of the film, studio executives were still uncomfortable with the idea of combining horror with comedy, as evidenced by the notes Joel Schumacher received from Warner Brothers about his teenaged vampire film *The Lost Boys*. It took the success of his film and the box office earnings of the increasingly jokey Freddy Krueger movies before people began to recognize that it was possible for a horror movie to get laughs and still be scary. Nine years later, with the enormous success of *Scream*, the attitude in Hollywood turned full circle and it was now believed that for a horror movie to be successful it *had* to be both funny and scary.[6] Serious horror films became the exception rather than the norm, until the success of *The Sixth Sense* (1999) changed the rules all over again.

The notion of combining the two genres in this way is now so universally accepted that it's a little hard to believe

---

6 This trend found its creative peak not on movie screens but on television, where *Buffy the Vampire Slayer* and *Angel* managed to effortlessly combine the genres week after week with tremendously satisfying results.

that it shocked people just 20 years ago, but it's true. Its groundbreaking style is now so ubiquitous that it serves as proof that whenever people say something can't be done, it's only because they've never seen anyone do it before.

How It Happened

John Landis was just 19 when he first thought up the idea for *An American Werewolf in London*. Even at that early age, he was already working in Hollywood. He had started out in the mailroom at 20th Century Fox when he was 17, and he used the contacts he made there to get work as a stuntman in *The Charge of the Light Brigade* (1968) and Sergio Leone's masterpiece *Once Upon A Time In the West* (1969).[7] He became a production assistant on the 1970 Clint Eastwood WWII heist-comedy *Kelly's Heroes*. The film was shot on location in what was then Yugoslavia, and it was there that Landis witnessed a strange custom, which gave him the idea for his uniquely funny werewolf script.

While driving down a long, single-lane dirt road with a fellow crew member, Landis came upon a tribe of gypsies who were in the process of burying one of their own. What struck Landis as odd about the ceremony was that the coffin was being placed into the ground feet first and was wrapped with long strands of garlic. His Yugoslavian companion, a man named Sasha, told Landis that the gypsies were afraid that the man was "cursed" so he had to be buried in a way that would not allow him to escape from his grave and cause

---

7 His specialty was falling off of horses, a skill that was much in demand in both films.

mischief. Landis was struck silent by an odd thought. *What if the guy in the coffin really did escape from his grave?*

The idea of it seemed so absurd that Landis instantly recognized the humorous potential of a story in which a guy just like himself was thrown into a strange, supernatural horror movie straight out of the old Universal Studios. But he didn't want it to become a spoof, where everything was played for laughs. It would be first and foremost a horror movie that was meant to scare the pants off of anyone who saw it, but the film would at the same time acknowledge the absurdity of its own plot and have some fun with its main characters.

With this in mind, he wrote a script and sent it to his contacts in the business. The script was funny enough to get him jobs for other projects, but the unanimous consensus among those who read it was that it would never get made.

Landis put the script aside temporarily and went to work instead on a very small independent film that he put together by borrowing money from his family and friends. *Schlock* (1973)[8] was an affectionate send-up of ape movies *King Kong* and *Bela Lugosi Meets A Brooklyn Gorilla* (1952).[9] Not only did he write and direct the movie, he also stared as the title character, suffering the many indignities that come while

---

8 A reference to the fact that the film's main character was a missing link called the Shlockthropus, as well as to the kind of film Landis was parodying.

9 Despite the efforts of the infamous Edward D. Wood Jr, this is easily the worst film that Bela Lugosi ever appeared in, which is a judgment not to be taken lightly given the kind of movies the iconic actor appeared in at the end of his career.

10 But these indignities are minor compared to the ones he would have suffered had he starred in the film he had originally planned on making. Inspired by the success of *Deep Throat* (1972), Landis had considered making his directorial debut with an underground xxx adult feature, but he changed his mind when he learned that the distributors and theaters that handled these films were all owned and operated by the mafia.

wearing an ape costume,[10] which had been designed by a young make-up artist and special effects technician named Rick Baker.

Baker was no stranger to gorilla suits. As a teenager who had grown up obsessed with monster movies, he had long harbored an affection for ape costumes and had built and worn one for the first film he worked on, *The Incredible 2-Headed Transplant* (1971).[11] By that time he had also designed the costume for the title creature in *Octaman* (1971), the riveting tale of a half-man, half-octopus hybrid running amok in a trailer park.

The film did little to further Landis' career. It was funny[12] and well made for a film with such a miniscule budget, but its jokes and references were not ones that mainstream audiences could really appreciate. Landis had made the mistake of making a film that was too "inside" to appeal to people who hadn't spent their childhood obsessed with B-movies.

It would be another four years before he got a chance to make another movie. This one was called *The Kentucky Fried Movie* (1977), and it consisted of a series of sketches and comic vignettes without any kind of plot to string them together.[13] Unlike similar sketch films made during that

---

11 An early film in Bruce Dern's career that shouldn't be confused with *The Thing With Two Heads* which was released a year later and starred Ray Milland and Rosie Grier as the titular monstrosity. Both films are highly recommended for fans of inept filmmaking, but *The Thing With Two Heads* wins out as the better one if only for its incredibly memorable tagline: "They transplanted a white bigot's head onto a soul brother's body!"

12 Its best moment is a hilarious scene where Schlock meets and befriends a beautiful blind woman who assumes the large hairy creature is a big dog. She starts playing a game of fetch with him, and he grows increasingly angrier each time she throws away the stick he has just gone out of his way to retrieve for her.

13 The film was written by two brothers, Jerry and David Zucker, and their friend Jim Abrahams. Together these three would later experience enormous success as the writers and directors of *Airplane!* (1980), a film whose impact on the comedy genre is still being felt today.

period, such as *The Groove Tube* (1974), *Tunnel Vision* (1976) and *Loose Shoes* (1980), *Kentucky Fried Movie* had the unique advantage of actually being funny. Even though many of its jokes and references are highly dated today, it still remains a very entertaining comedy to watch.[14]

It was thanks to *Kentucky Fried Movie* that Landis got the attention of Matty Simmons, the publisher of the then-popular *National Lampoon* magazine, who was producing a film based on the collegiate experiences of several of the *Lampoon*'s writers. He asked Landis to read the script and tell him what he thought of it. Landis thought it was funny but had some concerns about some of its content. It turned out that Simmons had been troubled by the very same details, and so he decided Landis was the perfect man for the job. Only 27 when he got the assignment, Landis brought a youthful exuberance to his role as the film's director that had an infectious effect on his cast and crew. When *National Lampoon's Animal House* (1978) was released, it was more

Following *Schlock*, both Landis and Baker did not abandon their affection for apes or ape costumes. An ape played an important part in Landis' *Trading Places* (1983), and many of his other films have included some kind of visual reference to our primate friends. Baker would later design and wear the suit used by the makers of the 1976 remake of *King Kong* when Carlo Rambaldi's proposed life-sized mechanical version of Kong didn't work out. He also designed the ape costumes that appeared in *The Incredible Shrinking Woman* (1981), *Greystoke: The Legend of Tarzan, Lord of the Apes* (1984), *Harry and the Hendersons* (1987), *Gorillas in the Mist* (1988), as well as the remakes of *Mighty Joe Young* (1998) and *Planet of the Apes* (2001).

than a breakthrough hit—it was a phenomenon. It quickly became the top-grossing comedy of all time and turned its star, John Belushi, into a Hollywood icon.

Now the young King of Hollywood,[15] Landis followed up his success with another hit movie. *The Blues Brothers* (1980) was a big-budget action-comedy-musical based around characters that Belushi and Dan Aykroyd had created on *Saturday Night Live*. It was a funny, chaotic film that ended with a completely over-the-top car chase that remains the pinnacle cinematic art-form in its execution, and its popularity gave Landis the clout he needed to get the green light to make any film his heart desired.

This was finally his chance to make *An American Werewolf in London* exactly the way he had always wanted to, and Landis eagerly took advantage it.

One of the first things Landis did when he started production on the film was call his old collaborator Rick Baker and ask him if he wanted to work on the film's special effects. Baker was both very intrigued and intimidated by the challenges that Landis was proposing to him in his descriptions of what he wanted. The first challenge was the creature itself. Landis didn't want the werewolf to walk on two legs like Lon Chaney Jr. had in *The Wolf Man* (1941) or Oliver Reed had in *The Curse of the Werewolf* (1961); he instead wanted the monster to be totally inhuman—a snarling, four-legged hell-beast that bore no resemblance to a man. Baker didn't know if he could pull that off, but it was a minor problem

---

14 Landis must have enjoyed making *Kentucky Fried Movie* because he returned to the format a decade later with the even funnier *Amazon Women on the Moon* (1987).

15 A position he shared at the time with Steven Spielberg, whose biggest flop, *1941* (1979), was a blatant attempt to recapture the magic of *Animal House*.

compared to Landis' other demand. He wanted the scene where David, the main character, first transforms into the wolf to take place in a well-lit room, without any dissolves or cutaways. No matter what happened to David, Landis wanted to see it happen on-screen. Baker was certain that there was no way this could be done using the traditional methods, all of which depended heavily on editing and well-placed shadows to hide a special effect's tricks and seams. This meant that not only would he have to invent a completely new method to get the job done because everything needed to be done on-screen, he needed to execute it perfectly. Baker told Landis he would do it.[16]

When it came to casting the film, Landis went more by instinct than by the more traditional methods. None of the leads were required to audition or read for their roles. Landis just met with them and decided who he wanted. The part of David went to David Naughton, who was best known at the time as the young man in a very popular Dr. Pepper soft drink commercial whose jingle was as infectious as the bubonic plague.[17] Though he was almost 30 at the time, Naughton still looked young enough to play a young college student.[18] The only question actor Griffin Dunne was asked

---

16 Baker took the challenge so seriously that he once proposed that the transformation scene be shot in a single take without any edits at all, which is not unlike a person who is planning on juggling eight chainsaws while balancing a grand piano on his nose suggesting that he try it while riding a unicycle. Landis nixed the idea, arguing, rightly, that the scene would be much more dramatic if it were filmed in a series of shorter shots rather than just one long one.

17 "I'm a pepper, he's a pepper, she's a pepper, wouldn't you like to be a pepper too?"

18 Which he had just done that same year in Walt Disney's *Midnight Madness* (1980), a film famous today for featuring the big screen debut of Michael J. Fox.

during his interview with Landis was "Are you claustropho-bic?" Dunne said he wasn't and got the part, wondering why Landis would ask that particular question.

Out of all the actors in the cast, the only famous name belonged to the beautiful English actress Jenny Agutter, who played Alex, the nurse who falls in love with the doomed young David. At the age of 29, she was already an acting vet-eran who had been working steadily since she was 12. At the time she was best known for her roles in *Walkabout* (1971), *Logan's Run* (1976) and *Equus* (1977).

At the time, Griffin Dunne wasn't the only member of his family leaving a mark in scary movie history. A year later, his sister Dominique starred as the Freeling's oldest daughter in Tobe Hooper's smash hit *Poltergeist* (1982). Unfortunately, Dominique's career was cut short when she was murdered by an abusive ex-boyfriend just a few months after *Poltergeist*'s release. The trial that followed her death, and the eventual release of her murderer after he served just a few years in prison, inspired their father, Dominick Dunne, a film producer, to start a new career as one of America's premier true-crime journalists. When Dominique's young costar, Heather O'Rourke, died six years later after filming the third and last sequel in the *Poltergeist* series, an urban legend began to spread that the men and women involved with the making of these films were cursed. Adding fuel to this speculation were the untimely deaths of actors Will Sampson and Julian Beck, who both appeared in *Poltergeist II: The Other Side* (1986). But, like all urban legends, the story of a *Poltergeist* curse has little to do with the facts and more to do with people trying to make sense out of a series of unfortunate coincidences.

But as easy as it had been for Landis to cast the film, there were some bureaucratic problems with his choices. In order to film in England as he wanted, Landis needed permits from the British branch of the performers union Actor's Equity for his American actors. Since Naughton was playing the film's lead role, the union gave him his permit without a problem, but they hesitated to give one to Griffin Dunne, as they felt an actor who already belonged to British Equity could be given the smaller role. Landis stood firm in his decision to cast Dunne and went so far as to go to France to scout locations for *An American Werewolf in Paris*, which is what the film would have been called if the union hadn't relented and given Dunne the necessary permit.

But before they went to England, Naughton and Dunne had to meet with Rick Baker and his crew in October 1980 and submit themselves to the process of having molds of their faces and hands made. It was then that Dunne learned why Landis wanted to know if he was claustrophobic—if he had been, there was no way he would have gotten through the whole mold-making operation. Baker used these molds to create the werewolf and the makeup that would be used on Dunne as his undead character, Jack, slowly starts to decompose. Even though Dunne's makeup throughout the film did not seem as spectacular as the complicated werewolf effects, it was probably more effective. If you were to ask people about details they remember from the film, many of them would likely include the small flap of loose skin that wobbles back and forth during Jack and David's first meeting after being savaged by the werewolf. It was small, but these important details made Baker's work on the film so extraordinary.

Filming began in February 1981. Landis didn't believe in rehearsing, so a lot of what happened before the cameras was completely spontaneous. The actors gave fresher and more genuine performances that were not usually found in horror movies. One of the most effective scenes occurs at the very beginning of the film when Jack and David are walking down a road in Northern England discussing Jack's obsession with a vapid, but very well-built, young woman. When Dunne and Naughton found themselves laughing uncontrollably as the scene was being filmed, the camera captured a moment that would have been impossible to fake. Right from the start it becomes clear that they are not the typical heroes of a horror film. They're just regular guys in an uncomfortable situation.

But it was not all fun and games. Landis' screenplay required that Naughton be placed in some extremely uncomfortable situations. The most dangerous moment is when David wakes up naked in the wolves' den at a London zoo after his first night as the werewolf. For the scene Naughton was actually placed naked inside a cage with real wolves and told to figure out a way to get out. Think of this the next time you hear someone talk about spoiled movie stars. When have you ever been required to stand naked among a group of very dangerous and highly unpredictable animals as a part of your job?[19]

And then there was the most important scene in the film—the legendary transformation scene. It took six days to

---

19 Being naked with the wolves wasn't Naughton's only uncomfortable moment involving nudity on the film. The producers of the film had only been able to secure permission to shoot at the zoo for the few hours in the morning before it opened to the public. This wasn't enough time to get all of the shots they needed, so they kept on filming as people started entering the zoo. These people can be seen in several of the scenes in which David appears naked around the zoo. Luckily, the crew was able to shoot everything they needed without any hassle.

shoot because of the long waiting period between setups. Baker and his crew[20] had done such a good job of building the effects that many of them were shot in quick, single takes without any technical difficulties. Baker would later admit to feeling conflicted about spending months working on and building his meticulous props for just a few minutes filming.

One prop that was needed more than once was the werewolf itself. Baker decided to design the creature as a puppet, whose back legs would never be seen in a shot, since that would be where the puppeteer stood and operated it. Baker based the design of the wolf on his dog Bosco, but he deliberately sculpted its face to look more demonic. Though Landis would later insist that he included too many shots of the creature in the finished film, there are only a handful of shots where one gets a clear sense of what the wolf really looks like.

Landis' choice to avoid the standard movie clichés with the werewolf is another reason why the film stands out as much as it does. There is something much more primal and frightening about the idea of transforming into a completely different species rather than just sprouting sharper canines and claws and growing hair all over your body. The traditional Hollywood werewolf is a clear metaphor for the savage beast that lurks inside all of us, but the werewolf in Landis' film is closer in spirit to Franz Kafka's Gregor Samsa, a man who wakes up one morning and discovers he has transformed into a cockroach. With the traditional werewolf story, David would somehow be responsible for the murders

---

20 *An American Werewolf* marked the first time Baker ever worked on a film with anything other than a single assistant. He had five other people working with him, all of whom were just fans who had admired his previous work.

the werewolf commits, as if its crimes could easily be interpreted as part of his own unconscious desire. However, Landis turns David into a creature incapable of human consciousness, and as a result—like Kafka's pathetic protagonist—his fate is much more tragic and existentially bleaker.

But rather than dwelling on the most depressing aspects of the story, Landis went out of his way to mine humor out of some of the plot's darkest moments. For example, in the scene in the adult movie theater[21] where David is met by the now almost-skeletal Jack,[22] who introduces his friend to all of the people he murdered the night before, everyone is cheerfully brainstorming ways David could kill himself before he transforms again. Even though Jack is eager for his friend's suicide, he is quick to reject any method that might result in unnecessary suffering.

For the film's ending, Landis and Baker went all out in creating an orgy of chaos and violence. Not just satisfied with simply having the werewolf bite off a man's head, Landis wanted to show the anarchy that would result if such a creature really were to suddenly appear in a major urban center.[23] The werewolf itself only kills two men, but many more die in the sudden maelstrom his presence creates. Vehicles crash into each other and people are thrown through windshields

---

21 Which is showing a uniquely horrible sex comedy called *See You Next Wednesday,* which Landis shot specifically for the sequence. The title of the film is a good luck charm that has appeared in almost all of his movies. Taken from a line in Stanley Kubrick's *2001: A Space Odyssey* (1968), it was the title Landis had attached to a film idea he had been nursing since he was teenager. Though he never made the film, he has admitted that aspects of it have appeared in his other movies.

22 An effect achieved by using a puppet whose mouth movements were controlled by Griffin Dunne himself.

23 In this case, London's Piccadilly Circus.

and run over and crushed by cars,[24] as the werewolf walks along and growls menacingly at all it passes.

Once again Landis is able to create a scene that works by emphasizing the reality over the fantasy. The simple presence of the monster causes more damage and a higher bodycount than the monster could ever hope to achieve by itself. What also rings true is how quickly the monster is dispatched. The police corner it in an alley where it is confronted by a tearful Alex, who now knows that David wasn't crazy when he told her what was happening to him. For a moment it seems that the man inside the wolf recognizes her, but this lasts for just a second before the wolf lunges towards her and is killed in a hail of gunfire.[25] Alex starts to weep[26] and David's body is seen lying naked on the ground before the screen cuts to the film's end credits. The film's resolution is clear and uncomplicated. For the common good David had to die and killing him required nothing more than a few standard-issue bullets.

In a film in which verisimilitude is given so much respect, Landis is also quick to experiment with an occasionally dreamlike narrative. During David's stay in the hospital he is tormented by nightmares that anticipate the horror he is about to face, but the most memorable and powerful dream

---

24 If you look quickly you can spot Landis reliving his old stuntman days in a shot where he is hit by a car and thrown through a store window.

25 In the movie theater David asks Jack if he needs to use silver bullets to kill himself and Jack responds, "Oh please, be serious."

26 If the film has a flaw, it is in the character of Alex. Jenny Agutter is a delight in every scene she appears in, but Landis' script fails in creating believable motivations for her actions throughout the film, such as when she decided to take a strange—possibly psychotic—man home, and also her bizarre non-reaction when he told her about waking up that morning naked in a zoo.

is one that has absolutely nothing to do with his becoming a werewolf. In it, David is at home with his family in America, when a group of demons dressed in Nazi regalia bursts through the front door and murders everyone in front of him before cutting his throat. David wakes up and finds his nurse, Alex, in the room with him. She asks him if he wants her to open up the drapes and let in some light and he agrees. When she goes to the window, she is attacked and killed by one of the S.S. demons in what is probably the biggest jump-scare in the whole movie. While it would be easy to dismiss this sequence as superfluous in an already scary movie, it does serve a purpose as it comes right before the moment when Jack first visits David. Landis claims he was invoking the same effect Spanish filmmaker Luis Bunuel used in his classic *The Discreet Charm of the Bourgeoisie* (1972), where the narrative is filled with so many dream sequences that it becomes hard for the viewer to keep track of what is real and what is not, and it isn't an accident that when David sees his mutilated friend in front of him that we are quick to assume that this is another nightmare. It is not until the moment David finally becomes the werewolf that we learn that Jack truly isn't just a figment of David's imagination.

To give the film an added level of self-awareness, Landis also had fun playing with the film's soundtrack. Three different versions of the classic song "Blue Moon" appear in the film: Bobby Vinton's elegantly arranged take on the song plays over the opening credits; Sam Cooke's more soulful version plays during David's first painful transformation; and The Marcels' bombastic doo-wop cover of the song, which is strangely upbeat in contrast to the ending, plays during the end credits. Also included on the soundtrack is Creedence Clearwater Revival's "Bad Moon Rising," which plays during a montage showing David trying to pass the time when Alex leaves him alone in her flat, and Van Morrison's "Moondance" which is heard during the film's obligatory sex scene. Landis attempted to get the rights to use the Cat Steven's[27] song "Moonshadow," but the devoutly religious singer refused to let his song appear in the film because he believed werewolves were real and feared that they might come after him if he did.[28]

After filming wrapped in March, Landis sped through the post-production process and had the film ready for release by August. As noted earlier, the film was not met with universal acclaim upon its release. Many people were put off by its stubborn refusal to follow the dictates of either of the two genres it seemed to aspire to. Serious horror fans were offended by the film's humorous tone, and comedy fans were disgusted by the gory special effects and annoyed by its casual attitude towards violence.[29] Still, it did okay at the box office, earning $30 million, which was enough to triple its $10 million cost, making it a minor hit for PolyGram, the company that produced it.

---

27 AKA Youssef Islam, as he is known today.

28 Bizarrely, no attempt was made to secure the rights to Warren Zevon's classic "Werewolves of London," even though it was clearly *a propos*.

29 Following the grim seriousness of the films of the 1970s, many people were offended by the idea of attaching any kind of humor to cinematic violence. Despite the best efforts of Landis and the madmen of Monty Python, it wouldn't be until the early 1990s—thanks mostly to the effort of Quentin Tarantino—that most people were willing to admit that— if done right—violence could be as rich a source of humor as anything else.

The Aftermath

John Landis followed up *An American Werewolf in London* with the comedy *Trading Places* (1983), a film that had originally been written for Gene Wilder and Richard Pryor as a follow-up to the enormous success of their 1980 hit *Stir Crazy*. When Pryor dropped out of the film, a young, new, black comedian making a splash on *Saturday Night Live* named Eddie Murphy was given the role. Fearing that starring with Wilder would result in unwanted comparisons to Pryor, Murphy had him replaced by Dan Aykroyd and the resulting film was the second biggest hit of Landis' career, after *Animal House*.

That same year Landis and Baker were asked to reunite by singer Michael Jackson, a huge fan of *An American Werewolf*, to make the video for the title track off of his new album "Thriller." At Michael's urging, Landis created what was closer to a 20-minute mini-movie than a traditional rock video, one that—like *An American Werewolf*—combined genuine terror with tongue-in-cheek humor. MTV promoted the video's debut as if it was the second coming and, when it aired, it was judged to be the greatest music video of all time. A home video about the making of the video was released, and it was—for a few years, at least—the top-selling videotape of all time.[30]

But despite all of this success, not everything was going well for Landis. In 1982, he along with fellow directors Steven Spielberg, Joe Dante and George Miller, contributed a segment

---

30 An achievement somewhat mitigated by the fact that when the tape was released very few videos were priced to sell to the average consumer.

to a feature film version of Rod Sterling's classic fantasy anthology series *The Twilight Zone*. While the other directors filmed new versions of classic episodes,[31] Landis wrote and directed an original segment about a white bigot who finds himself transported into the body of a Vietnamese man during the Vietnam War. Playing the bigot was well-known character actor Vic Morrow,[32] who in one scene was required to run down a battlefield with two young child actors under his arms as the three of them were pursued by a passing helicopter. The two young actors, Renee Chen and My-ca Le, were not supposed to be there, since labor laws did not allow children to work during the hours the scene was filmed at, but their parents (who had been paid with cash) allowed the crew to use them. As the scene was being shot, Landis and his crew watched with horror when one of the explosions from the ground caused the helicopter to spin out of control and crash into the ground, killing the pilot, as well as Morrow and the two children.

Deadly accidents on sets are more common than many people would want to believe, but this accident earned far more publicity than normal because it involved both a well-known actor[33] and two children who should never have even been on set, much less involved in such a dangerous scene. In June 1983, Landis and several others were indicted by a Los Angeles grand jury on charges of involuntary manslaughter.

---

31 Strangely, many critics at the time did not realize this and reported that of the four segments, only Miller's was based on an old episode from the series.

32 Best remembered today for his starring role on the WWII series *Combat* and for being the father of the Academy Award-nominated actress Jennifer Jason Leigh.

33 As opposed to an unknown stuntman.

The case went to trial three years later in 1986 and lasted for nine months before Landis and the others were acquitted of the charges. In the end, the jury decided that even though Landis and the crew had been wrong to illegally put the two children in harm's way, there was no way anyone could have known that the helicopter would crash. It was, they decided, a very tragic accident.

Landis was extremely (and understandably) shaken by what happened on the set of *The Twilight Zone: The Movie* (1983), and had told friends that he didn't know if he could ever direct again. Some wondered if the accident would get him blacklisted by the studios. In the years that followed he would have just one more hit with *Coming to America*. The rest of his films ended up being disappointments, such as *Spies Like Us* (1985), *Three Amigoes* (1986) and *Beverly Hills Cop III*, or outright bombs such as *Into the Night* (1985), *Oscar* (1991) and *The Stupids* (1996). Only once did he attempt to recreate the success of *An American Werewolf* when he made the vampire comedy *Innocent Blood*[34] (1992) starring Anthony LaPaglia and *La Femme Nikita*'s (1990) Anne Parillaud. In it, Parillaud played a French vampire who chooses to satisfy her need for blood by only feeding on criminals and gangsters, but her good intentions are undone when one of her victims survives and becomes a vampire intent on using his new supernatural abilities to rise to the top of the criminal underworld. What had worked so well a decade earlier didn't work now. *Innocent Blood*'s script was too broad and unfocused, and its two leads weren't charismatic enough to obscure the film's

34 Which in some parts of the world was released as *A French Vampire in America.*

Baker himself flourished after the release of *An American Werewolf*. Thanks largely to his work on the film, the Academy of Motion Picture Arts and Sciences decided in 1982 to implement a new Academy Award for Special Achievement in Makeup Effects, which he won and would go on to win—as of this writing—five more times (for *Harry and the Hendersons* (1987), *Ed Wood* (1995), *The Nutty Professor* (1997), *Men in Black* (1998) and *How the Grinch Stole Christmas* (2001)). He would also earn nominations for his work on *Greystoke: The Legend of Tarzan, Lord of the Apes* (1985), *Coming to America* (1988) and *Life* (2000).

flaws. It sank without a trace from theaters and is barely remembered today.

Landis had nothing to do with *An American Werewolf in Paris* (1997), a sequel made almost 20 years after the original. In fact, no one connected to the original movie had anything to do with the sequel. Landis had deliberately ended the first film so there wouldn't be a sequel, and this effort had to strain to show any connections to the original.[35] It lacked all of the originality of the first film and was filled with computer-generated werewolf effects that looked cool, but had none of the visceral impact of Rick Baker's groundbreaking work. It was a completely unnecessary project whose creation was due only to a desire to capitalize on what was now considered a classic horror film by fans of the genre.

---

35 Even though its lead female character is the French-raised daughter of David and Alex, this detail could have easily been changed and the film could have been released as a completely original movie.

The beast emerges. (David Naughton in
An American Werewolf in London)

Also Look For

Fans of *An American Werewolf in London* have been well
served by Universal's special edition DVD release of this classic film. Among its special features is a feature-length commentary by stars David Naughton and Griffin Dunne, a new,
half-hour interview with John Landis and several older documentaries shot when the movie was made in 1981. For
more of Landis, film buffs are advised to seek out Anchor
Bay's DVD release of his second film *Kentucky Fried Movie*,
which includes a commentary by Landis who is joined by the
film's writers, Jim Abrahams, and Jerry and David Zucker.

Big Hairy Deals

The Good

Obviously, *An American Werewolf in London* isn't the only scary movie that does justice to the business of lycanthropy, so here are five more werewolf flicks you should make an effort to find at your local video store.

1) ***Ginger Snaps* (2000):** A low-budget Canadian film that was obviously inspired by *An American Werewolf*, this is quite possibly the most entertaining scary movie to be made in the past decade. Karen Walton's screenplay ingeniously juxtaposes lycanthropy with puberty in this tale of Bridget and Ginger, two teenaged Goth sisters who are forced to grow up, both figuratively and literally, when Ginger is bitten by a strange animal and is overcome with a burgeoning sexuality she did not know she possessed. Two highly enjoyable sequels followed in 2004.

2) ***The Howling* (1981):** Released around the same time as *An American Werewolf*, this is the second best werewolf movie of 1981. Directed by Joe Dante from a script by John Sayles, this is a fun B-movie starring Dee Wallace Stone, best known as the mother in *ET the Extra-Terrestrial*, as a reporter who stumbles upon a colony of popular character actors who all just happen to get a bit hairy when the full moon is out. It was followed by seven sequels, none of which were at all connected to the original or worth seeing.

3) *Dog Soldiers* **(2002):** A British film, *Dog Soldiers* was written and directed by Neil Marshall and tells the tale of a group of special-forces soldiers who are forced to deal with an enemy they never previously could have imagined. Well made and refreshingly free of computer-generated effects, the film has received little attention in North American, except among genre fans, but it is well worth keeping an eye out for.

4) *The Wolf Man* **(1941):** The classic "man to beast" original starring Lon Chaney Jr. This is the film that helped to create the mythology that so many other films would later follow. Among the classic horror films made by the studio during that period, it ranks third just behind the first two Frankenstein films at the top of the list. Creighton Chaney was forced to use Lon Chaney

The other side of Larry Talbot. (Lon Chaney Jr. in *The Wolf Man*)

Jr. as his name because Universal wanted to exploit the public's affection for his famous father, "The Man of a 1000 Faces."

5) *The Curse of the Werewolf* **(1961):** After reinventing the horror genre with their new takes on the Dracula and Frankenstein legends, England's Hammer Films decided it was time to tackle the Wolf Man. Like all of the movies made by the hardworking studio, special emphasis was made on the gothic Victorian sets and the plunging necklines of the female actresses (Yvonne Romain's being particularly noteworthy). Still, the film is made memorable thanks to the lead performance of famous British bad boy Oliver Reed, who somehow manages to look more refined and civilized in his wolf makeup than he does without it.

A typical Hammer pose. (Oliver Reed and Catherine Feller in *Curse of the Werewolf*)

The Not-So-Good

It seems a bit too easy to call these movies dogs, but if the collar fits....

1) *An American Werewolf in Paris* (1997): Sixteen years is a long time to wait for a sequel, but in the case of this particular film, it wasn't nearly long enough.

2) *Monster Dog* (1984): As bad as this film is, at least it has the courage to admit it in its own title (even if that wasn't exactly what the filmmakers had intended). This ineptly made Italian production features that rock-and-roll bogey-man, Alice Cooper, in his only starring role.[1] He plays Victor Raven (this is a stretch), a rock-and-roll star who, due to a familial curse, turns into the title creature, which is essentially Cooper wearing a laughably bad Great Dane mask made out of paper mache. Cheap and boring, this is the kind of movie horror fans feel compelled to see, only to regret it once they have.

3) *Frankenstein Meets the Wolf Man* (1943): After becoming a star playing Dracula, Bela Lugosi was offered the part of the monster in the first Universal Frankenstein movie, but he refused it, insulted by the idea of playing a part that had no lines and required so much makeup. As a result, an unknown English character actor named Boris Karloff got

---

1 He has also had smaller roles in *Prince of Darkness* (1987), *Wayne's World* (1992) and *Freddy's Dead: The Final Nightmare* (1991), but—by far—his scariest motion picture appearance has to have been his duet with a calcified Mae West in the truly horrific musical comedy *Sextette* (1978).

the part and made film history. Lugosi grew to regret his mistake and tried to rectify it by taking the part the next time it was offered to him. He got his chance in *Frankenstein Meets the Wolf Man*, and once again fate played him a cruel blow. In the script, the monster is blinded at the beginning of the film and Lugosi played the part as it was intended; however, the producers decided during the film's editing to cut out all references to the monster's blindness, and Lugosi's performance no longer made any sense. Thanks largely to this, the film is considered by most to be the worst of the classic Universal horror films.

The lamest werewolf makeup of all time. (Jack Nicholson in *Wolf*)

4) *Wolf* **(1994):** Directed by Mike Nichols and starring Jack Nicholson, by all rights this film should have been in my first list of werewolf movies. Yet even the enormous talents of these two men were not enough to save the project from a weak script, along with Nichols' obvious distrust for the genre he was working in. In the film, Nicholson plays an aging executive on a slow decline who suddenly turns his life around when he becomes a werewolf and loses his inhibitions. What he doesn't know is that he's not the only employee at the company he works for who is also benefiting from this primal lifestyle. As fun as this concept could be, Nichols stubbornly refuses to delve into the plot's darkest reaches, and saddles Nicholson with the lamest werewolf makeup in film history (essentially just some fangs and a pair of muttonchop sideburns).[2] A sad case of what might have been.

5) *Silver Bullet* **(1985):** A good rule to follow if you're going to watch a lot of horror films is to avoid any movie based on a Stephen King story whose screenplay has also been written by Stephen King. *Silver Bullet* is the film largely responsible for this rule. Based on his novella *Cycle of the Werewolf*, the film is a derivative affair, completely lacking in the creativity that can so often be found in films adapted from King's work by other screenwriters. The film isn't terrible, just bland and unimaginative.

---

2 Provided, shockingly, by Rick Baker, who—it must be assumed—was working under strict orders from Nichols.

4
The Dream Franchise

A Nightmare On Elm Street

Fred Krueger was not someone you wanted living in
your neighborhood.

He was rude,
he was obnoxious,
he told bad jokes
and he was a serial killer
who specialized in murdering children.

When the authorities finally caught him,
the people who lived on Elm Street
thought they were now safe,
but serious and illegal mistakes were made
during the investigations of his crimes
and the judge was forced to let this madman go free.

He returned to Elm Street,
but he was not greeted back with open arms.
Instead, his neighbors gathered together
and burned him alive.

Years later
their children are tormented by nightmares so real
that to have one means risking never waking up.

Nancy Thompson is one of those kids
and she alone knows the truth.

Krueger has returned from the grave
to claim revenge on the children of his murderers,
but he has not arisen in the real world.
He has resurrected himself in the land of dreams,
where he has the power to make the rules
and be as cruel as his twisted heart desires...

This is What We Know

No one knows anything.
   —William Goldman, *Adventures in the Screen Trade*

What screenwriter William Goldman[1] meant when he wrote those words in his 1983 book about the film industry was very simple. No matter how many theories people in Hollywood come up with to explain one film's success and another film's failure, the truth is that no one really has any idea why certain films do well and others do not. The anecdotes that illustrate the sage truth of Goldman's explanation for Hollywood's follies are numerous. For example, some of the executives at 20th Century Fox considered halting production on a movie being made by George Lucas called *Star Wars* (1977) and using some of the effects footage shot for a Saturday morning kid's show. The executives at Paramount fought vociferously with Francis Ford Coppola over his decision to cast Marlon Brando—who was considered an expensive has-been—and Al Pacino—who was unknown at the time—in *The Godfather* (1972). Miramax was forced by its parent company, Walt Disney, to halt its development of two Peter Jackson films based on the highly popular *Lord of the Rings* books because the proposed budgets for the two movies were too high.

These are just three out of a thousand similar behind-the-scenes tales, but they all illustrate the same point: any time a filmmaker attempts to take a risk and tries to create something groundbreaking, there are going to be people who

---

1 Whose scary movie credits include *The Stepford Wives* (1975), *Magic* (1978), *Misery* (1990) and *Dreamcatcher* (2003).

try to stop them. Why? Because no one knows anything. With the benefit of hindsight, the executives mentioned above were all clearly wrong as they fought to halt production on some of the most successful movies in film history, but the truth is that their doubts were perfectly reasonable at the time. A lot of the early *Star Wars* footage was awful and bore little resemblance to the finished film; Marlon Brando at that point in his career had starred in a dozen flops and Al Pacino had only appeared in two other movies and was half a foot shorter than James Caan, the actor hired to play his brother; and long before the *Lord of the Rings* trilogy, expensive Tolkienesque-fantasy films such as *Krull* (1983), *Legend* (1985) and *Willow* (1988) had done very poorly at the box office.

It is because of this uncertainty, which is inherent in the business of moviemaking, that when a groundbreaking film is successful, the natural impulse is to follow it up with a sequel. In some cases this isn't possible, but much more often executives who tried to stop the first film get made are only too happy to produce sequels of rapidly diminishing quality until every last nickel has been squeezed out of a franchise. What this means is that often the reputation of a great film is tarnished by a series of exploitative sequels that are seldom made by the same creative team responsible for the original. Just look at what happened to *Rocky* (1976). Today, thanks to a series of increasingly horrible sequels, few people remember that the first film was actually nominated for 10 Oscars[2] and won for Best Picture, Best Director[3] and Best

---

2 Including—as hard as it is to believe today—nominations for Best Actor and Best Original Screenplay for Sylvester Stallone.

3 John G. Avidsen.

Film Editing.[4] Instead they are more likely to recall Mr. T's "performance" as Clubber Lang in *Rocky III* (1982), that same movie's stridently-80s theme song "Eye of the Tiger"[5] and the absurd Cold War politics of *Rocky IV*[6] (1985).

And if you're wondering what this all has to do with *A Nightmare On Elm Street* (1984), then you've never heard The Fat Boys perform "Are You Ready For Freddy?" from the soundtrack to Part 4: The Dream Master, or played with a Freddy Krueger hand puppet or remembered how annoying it was to watch *Freddy's Dead: The Final Nightmare*[7] while wearing those cheap cardboard 3D glasses.

The following is a tale of how a low-budget horror movie no one wanted to make resulted in a mini-industry of inferior sequels that is still profitable today, 20 years later, and how it helped transform a small, New York-based distribution company into a major Hollywood entity.

This is the story of a very charismatic monster who sold out and cashed.

How It Happened

There are few careers in the history of scary movies as interesting as Wes Craven's. He is a man who has made films so unique and powerful that they have gone on to

---

4 Richard Halsey and Scott Conrad.

5 Brought to us by those one-hit wonders, Survivor.

6 A film so over-the-top in its anti-Soviet hysteria that historians will someday wonder if it was written by an extremely patriotic child.

7 Which—like all horror sequels that insist they are the final installment in a series—wasn't.

revolutionize the horror movie genre or—at the very least— revitalize it. But at the same time he has also made the kind of cheaply produced dreck that critics of the genre are quick to use as examples of its cultural inferiority. His filmography is an intriguing collection of classics and clunkers, and is a good example of how the unpredictability of the film business can greatly affect a director's career.

Wes Craven was born in Cleveland, Ohio, in the summer of 1939. His parents separated when he was a toddler and his father was dead by the time that Wes was four. His impoverished mother took comfort in the local Baptist church, whose fundamentalist view of the Bible forbade its parishioners to read comic books or go to the movies. Young Craven instead spent his time at the library where he read all of the classics. He carried this interest in literature all through his adolescence until finally he reached college and pursued a degree in writing and philosophy. He earned his masters in those subjects at John Hopkins University and went on to teach at Clarkson University in Potsdam, New York.

While he was teaching at the university, he was asked by a group of students to become the faculty advisor for their film club and, through working with them, he became intrigued with the idea of being a filmmaker. His moment of truth came when the head of the humanities program told him that it was time to forget about the film club and start making serious attempts to get published and earn his doctorate. Instead of following the man's advice, Craven quit his job and moved to New York City where he worked as a taxi driver until he got a job as a sound editor at a post-production company.

During this time he became friends with another wannabe filmmaker named Sean S. Cunningham. Together the two of them collaborated on *Together* (1971), a soft-core documentary about sexuality in the age of communal living. That film did little to advance their careers, but its follow-up would not only get them a lot of attention, it would make them infamous.

The Last House on the Left (1972) was a remake of Ingmar Bergman's *The Virgin Spring* (1960). The film's plot of a mother and father's revenge following the rape and murder of their daughter was not what made the film so controversial, but rather it was how the story was filmed. The movie was shot in a grainy-documentary style, without any of the glamour found in a similar Hollywood thriller. The movie did not cut away from the moments the audience would usually never be allowed to see; instead, it lingered on them until they quickly became impossible to watch. The film sent shock waves around the world. Never before had this kind of brutality been seen on-screen, and it made a huge return at the box office at the expense of turning Craven and Cunningham into pariahs in their industry[8] and even society at large.

People were disgusted by the film,[9] but this negative reception didn't stop the film from having an impact on the genre. The same documentary style, which conveys a very real sense that what you see is really happening, would later appear in Tobe Hooper's classic *The Texas Chainsaw*

---

8 As mentioned in the chapter on *Halloween*, Cunningham turned to children's films until he finally returned to horror movies with *Friday the 13th*.

9 Which was advertised with the classic tagline *To avoid fainting keep repeating "It's only a movie...It's only a movie...It's only a movie..."*

10 Also known as *I Spit On Your Grave*, this brutal movie was often singled out by film critic Roger Ebert whenever he was asked to name the worst film he had ever reviewed. Interestingly, Ebert was one of the only critics to respond enthusiastically to *The Last House on the Left*, and his extremely negative response to *Day of the Woman*—as suggested by Carol J. Clover in *Men, Women and Chainsaws*—seems to have had more to do with how the audience he was with responded to the film than the film itself.

Massacre (1974) and Meir Zarchi's equally controversial revenge drama *Day of the Woman* (1978).[10] Craven found himself in the odd position of being unable to find work after making a hit movie that had made a lot of money. Five years would pass before he got the chance to make another film, thanks to a call from a producer named Peter Locke, who wanted to make another film such as *Last House on the Left*. Craven proposed an idea that he had had after hearing about an inbred family of criminals who plagued the roads between Edinburgh and London in the 16th century. In *The Hills Have Eyes* (1977), a normal American family—traveling through a desert to get to a piece of property they had just recently inherited—is forced to stop and fight against a family of mutant cannibals in order to survive. The result was another moneymaker, but this time Craven was able to capitalize on his success.

His next film was *Stranger in Our House* (1978), which starred *The Exorcist*'s (1973) Linda Blair, and was the first of five TV movies he would make in the next 12 years. He followed that up with *Deadly Blessing* (1981), a film notable only for featuring the future superstar, Sharon Stone, in her

Craven's other TV efforts included *Invitation to Hell* (1984), a film in which soap opera diva Susan Lucci was typecast—if the rumors of her onset behavior are to be believed—as the Devil; *Chiller* (1985), a thriller about the possible metaphysical dangers of cryogenics; *Casebusters* (1986), a family film about kid detectives; and *Night Visions* (1990), a fairly typical serial killer movie. As well as directing these TV movies, Craven also directed several segments for the 1985 CBS revamp of the classic TV series, *The Twilight Zone*.

first speaking part. After that came the comic-book adaptation *Swamp Thing* (1982). By all accounts this production was plagued by location problems and an unreasonably meager budget, which resulted in a poorly designed costume for the title character and an inability for Craven to get all of the shots he needed to film. Fans of the popular comic were extremely disappointed with the result, and the film's failure led Craven to suffer through another professional drought.

All during that time Craven had worked hard to sell a script he had written called *A Nightmare On Elm Street*, but no one was interested in making it. Craven had first come up with the idea for the film in 1979—a killer who attacks people in their dreams—when he had read a story in the *Los Angeles Times* about a teenaged immigrant from Cambodia who was so afraid of one of his recurring nightmares that he refused to sleep. His parents sought medical help and gave him sleeping pills, which he pretended to take, while he secretly kept a pot of coffee in his room to keep him awake. Finally, while watching TV one night, the exhaustion proved too much for him and he fell asleep. His parents found him and carried him back to his bed. A short time later they heard a horrible scream come from his room and when they ran to see what was wrong, it was too late; the young man was dead, apparently scared to death by his dream. Over the course of six months, two more articles appeared in the same paper describing similar incidents that also involved young immigrants from Southeast Asia who died in their sleep after complaining about nightmares. The newspaper never connected the three stories together, but they inspired Craven to write the first *Nightmare* script.

Everyone who read the script felt that it wasn't scary and it didn't make any sense. In an era where simple-minded slasher movies dominated the horror landscape, the idea of a killer who existed only in his victim's unconscious imagination was simply too far out there for a typical studio executive to appreciate. Two years passed during which Craven couldn't get a job and started going broke. Reaching the point where he had to borrow money from a friend to pay his taxes, Craven jumped at the chance to direct a sequel to *The Hills Have Eyes*. But as badly as he needed the paycheck, Craven could not force himself to care about the sequel and his obvious disinterest in the project was evident on screen. In order to finish the film, he padded the running time by including long flashbacks to the original movie, a move that alienated fans and confused newcomers to the film. When it was released in 1985, the film was judged to be a disaster by nearly everyone who saw it.

It seemed as though Craven's worries were finally over when a producer named Robert Shaye agreed to make *A Nightmare On Elm Street*. Shaye was the founder of New Line Cinema, a small, New York-based distribution company that specialized in low-budget exploitation movies. Tired of simply distributing movies other people had made, Shaye had recently started producing his own projects.[11] *Nightmare* would be his sixth film.

Given a budget of $1.8 million, Craven went to work finding the cast and crew he needed to put the film together. For the part of Nancy Thompson, the film's brave heroine, he cast a 19-year-old actress named Heather Langenkamp, whose only previous experience at that point were some

---

11 Including John Waters' first dip into the mainstream, *Polyester* (1981), and an underrated horror movie called *Alone in the Dark* (1982).

scenes that had been cut out of Francis Ford Coppola's *The Outsiders* (1983) and *Rumble Fish* (1983). To play her parents, Craven cast John Saxon, a character actor who had a long history of appearing in exploitation movies, and Ronee Blakley, an eccentric actress best remembered today for her performance as the doomed country singer Barbara Jean in Robert Altman's *Nashville* (1975). For the part of Glen, Nancy's boyfriend, Craven cast a handsome unknown named Johnny Depp, who at that time had no previous acting experience.

For the part of the film's villain, Fred Krueger, Craven had initially intended to cast a burly stuntman in the role, but worried that they wouldn't be able to give the character the personality that he deserved. Krueger was different from the other maniacs that were seen on-screen in those days. He spoke to his victims. He taunted and played with them. Krueger wasn't some mute moron who hacked people up with a machete; he wanted to truly terrify them before he

After the unexpected success of *Pirates of the Caribbean: Curse of the Black Pearl* (2003), Johnny Depp has finally achieved the superstardom that film buffs have long believed he deserved, and—if Wes Craven is to be believed—there is a good chance he owes his remarkable success to the enthusiasm of a 15-year-old girl. According to Craven, he had narrowed down his choices for the part of Glen to four actors. Three were typical blond surfer types and the fourth was the dark-haired 20-year-old Depp. Unable to decide, Craven turned to his teenaged daughter Jessica and asked her who she thought should get the part. Jessica—who had been allowed to sit in on the auditions—was unequivocal in her response. "Johnny Depp," she insisted forcefully. Craven took her advice, cast Depp and an eventual superstar was born.

It is rumored the Craven named the character after a bully who tormented him as a kid. If this is true, it's not the first time a filmmaker may have attempted to get revenge on a former tormentor by naming a villain after them. When fans of the *Star Wars* films found copies of George Lucas' high school yearbook, they were shocked and delighted to discover that one of his fellow students was a brawny jock named Gary Vader.

gutted them with his homemade steel claws.[12] This was on his mind when a character actor named Robert Englund[13] came in to audition for the part. Englund was smaller than Craven had imagined, and too young, but he had a willingness to take the character further out into the darkness than most actors were comfortable with. It was because of this that Craven decided to take a chance and cast Englund in the role.[14]

Like most low-budget horror movie productions, the shoot on *Nightmare* was short and fast-paced. The special effects required for the nightmare sequences proved to be the trickiest elements to deal with. Some of the shots required extensive planning, and complicated sets needed to be built.

---

12 Craven based the idea for Freddy's famous steel claws on how large cave bears in the pre-historic era would use their long claws to hook and capture our primitive ancestors as they cowered inside of crevices in the earth.

13 Best known at the time for his portrayal of Willie, the good-natured alien on the popular mini-series—and eventually TV show—*V* (1983).

14 Also featured in the small part of the dream researcher is an actor and comedian named Charles Fleischer, who is most famous for his performance as the voice of Roger Rabbit in Robert Zemeckis' *Who Framed Roger Rabbit* (1988). He would later work with Craven again as the voice of the robot BB in the director's abysmal feature follow-up to *Nightmare, Deadly Friend* (1986).

For the deaths of Tina (Amanda Wyss) and Glen, a special revolving set was set up to create the effects of her being dragged across her bedroom ceiling, and the geyser of blood that erupts from the middle of his bed after he has been murdered had to be designed. The first scene went well, but the geyser proved problematic. The spewing water created an unexpected shift of weight in the delicately balanced room and caused it to turn and spray onto the crew and their equipment, temporarily shutting down production. But not all of the effects in the film were so complicated. Perhaps the most effective shot in the entire film is the one in which Freddy's face and hands stretch out of the wall above the bed Nancy is sleeping in. This extremely creepy effect was simply improvised with a simple piece of stretched spandex by special effects designer Jim Doyle when a previous idea had to be abandoned.

The shoot wasn't easy on the actors. Nick Corri, who played Tina's boyfriend Rod, tore up his feet by repeatedly running barefoot on hot pavement. Johnny Depp was almost hit by the television set that followed him through the hole in the bed in his death scene. Heather Langenkamp had the unenviable task of running barefoot on a set covered in flaming footprints. All of the scenes in Freddy's boiler room were shot in a part of an abandoned prison that was later condemned for containing too much asbestos.

Unlike other genre filmmakers, Craven wasn't afraid of paying homage to some of his favorite influences. In the film's opening scene he included a shot of a sheep in the boiler room as a nod to the Spanish filmmaker Luis Bunuel, and in another scene a window is broken when a tooth is thrown into it, a reference to Roman Polanski's scary movie,

The Tenant (1976). He also wasn't above throwing in the occasional self-conscious joke here and there, the funniest being the moment when Nancy looks at herself in the mirror and complains "Oh my god, I look 20 years old," a line that acknowledges the standard practice of casting older actors in teenaged roles.[15] He also included a scene from Sam Raimi's *The Evil Dead* (1983) as a response to the torn-up poster for *The Hills Have Eyes* that appeared in Raimi's film.[16] These nods towards pretension and postmodern irony would later become much more apparent in his future films.

At Robert Shaye's request, Craven moved the film's post-production from Los Angeles to New York. Shaye was not enthusiastic when he saw the first cut of the film. "Do you think we have a film here at all?" Craven recalled him asking. Their biggest argument came over the ending. Originally the film ended with Nancy walking out of her house after having just defeated Freddy in her dream and disappearing into a mysterious fog. Considered too esoteric, this was replaced by a scene where Nancy walks out of her house and discovers that her murdered mother and friends are no longer dead. Her mother waves goodbye in front of her house as she joins her friends in the convertible car they are driving in, only to discover—too late—that Freddy hasn't really been vanquished when the car's top starts to rise[17] and the vehicle starts to drive away under Freddy's control. Nancy then sees her mother who is just then—in a very memorable shot—

---

15 At the time Heather Langenkamp was a lot closer to being 20 than 15.

16 See the chapter on *Evil Dead II: Dead By Dawn* for a more detailed account of this playful game of one upmanship.

17 Its striped design matching Freddy's soiled sweater.

grabbed by Freddy's clawed hand and pulled through the small window in the middle of her front door. Shaye liked the shock at the end, but thought it would work more effectively on audiences if—when Nancy gets into the car—it wasn't Glen behind the wheel, but Freddy himself. Craven thought this was too obvious and managed to get his version in the final cut of the film.

Despite his reservations about the film's quality, Shaye opened the film on November 11, 1984,[18] on 125 screens, where it grossed $1.3 million during its first weekend. At a per screen average of $10,168, this was an extremely impressive showing for such a small film, making it an instant hit. It would go on to gross over $25.5 million, earning 14 times what it had cost to make.[19]

The Aftermath

Once again Wes Craven had a hit at the box office and once again it did little to improve his career. Shaye wanted to capitalize on *Nightmare*'s success by making an immediate sequel. Craven had no problem with this, but he reasonably expected to be monetarily rewarded for the first film's success. Shaye disagreed and started production on the sequel without Craven, assigning scriptwriting duties to David Chaskin[20] and

---

18 After previewing it in April on a double bill with Sam Raimi's *The Evil Dead* (1981).

19 The critical response to the film was mixed, some reviewers praised the film's imagination and scenes of genuine terror, while others dismissed it as just another horror movie for teenagers.

20 The sequel would be his first produced script and he later wrote the scary movies *The Curse* (1987) and *I, Madman* (1989).

the director's chair to Jack Sholder.[21] The deal that Craven had signed with New Line to make the first *Nightmare* required him to sign away the rights to the Freddy Krueger character, which meant that the company could go forward with the project in anyway it saw fit.

To add insult to injury, Craven was named in a lawsuit by a screenwriter who insisted that he had stolen elements from the man's screenplay and placed them into his script for *Nightmare*. Lawsuits similar to this one are fairly common in the movie business, and owing to the initial contract, New Line wasn't obligated to help Craven with his legal costs, so the director was put in the absurd position of having to defend the creation of a film series that he no longer had legal rights to.

On November 3, 1985, New Line released *A Nightmare On Elm Street 2: Freddy's Revenge*, advertising it with the tagline, "He's back, but he's not happy." It opened on 522 screens and earned almost $3 million its first weekend. It would go on to gross nearly $30 million overall, breaking the standard 60% rule.[22] Artistically, the film simply wasn't as successful as the original. Nancy was nowhere to be found in the film, which instead focused on a teenaged boy named Jesse Walsh (Mark Patton) who Freddy tries to possess so he can spread his mayhem into the waking world. The problem is that Jesse simply isn't as compelling a character as Nancy was and there's too little of Freddy to make up the difference. The only thing that sets the film apart and makes it interesting

---

21 Who had previously made *Alone in the Dark* for New Line and would later direct the excellent *The Hidden* (1987) as well as several direct-to-video genre films.

22 In most cases a studio can expect a sequel to earn about 60% of the first film's gross.

is a subtle gay subtext,[23] but this is not enough to make the film worth watching.

At the time of the first sequel's release, Craven had gone through his second divorce, been forced to deal with the lawsuit mentioned earlier and directed one of the worst films of his career. *Deadly Friend* (1986) was based on a novel by Diana Henstell and featured a screenplay by Bruce Joel Rubin.[24] The film marked Craven's first assignment with a major studio, Warner Brothers, and—along with his ongoing personal problems—he was forced to deal with a level of creative interference he had never suffered before and the film failed miserably.[25]

Following the failure of *Deadly Friend*, Craven and New Line managed to settle their differences. Craven collaborated with screenwriter and novelist Bruce Wagner[26] on the story for the third installment of the *Nightmare* franchise, but he did not direct the film. That job went instead to first-time director Chuck Russell.[27] Later on, another newcomer named Frank Darabont[28] would be brought in to also work on the script. Craven and Wagner set the film in an asylum where

---

23 In the film he has a girlfriend, but the idea that he might be in the closet is there if you look for it.

24 Who would later write the megahit *Ghost* (1990) and one of the best scary movies of the 1990s, *Jacob's Ladder* (1990).

25 The movie does have one memorable moment where the resurrected girl, played by a young Kristy Swanson, kills Anne Ramsey by throwing a basketball through her head, but even this scene is marred by poorly executed special effects.

26 Best known as the author of the Hollywood-based novel *Force Majeure* and the creator of the Oliver Stone-produced mini-series *Wild Palms* (1993).

27 Who would go on to make *The Blob* (1988), a fun remake of the Steve McQueen camp classic and the very successful Jim Carrey film *The Mask* (1994).

28 Who would make his directing debut with *The Shawshank Redemption* (1994).

the last surviving children of the men and women who killed Freddy Krueger are being treated for their horrific night-mares. Their script answered two questions left over from the first film—what happened to Nancy and why Freddy was such an evil bastard. It turns out that Nancy survived her encounter with Freddy and became a counselor for the tor-mented kids at the asylum, and Freddy was an evil bastard because he was literally a bastard. More specifically, he was the "bastard son of a 100 maniacs," the unwanted child of a gang rape suffered by a nurse at a mental hospital for the criminally insane.

The film was eventually titled *A Nightmare On Elm Street 3: Dream Warriors*, and—not surprisingly, considering the general level of talent involved behind the screen—it is con-sidered by many to be the second best or even—some would say—the best film of the original franchise. As a character, Freddy is best represented in this third film. Given more screen time, he is allowed to become more fully developed as a villain, without yet becoming the punch-line-spewing Catskills comedian with one-liners that he would morph into in the following three features. The film opened in March of 1987 on 1,343 screens across North America—over 10 times as many theaters as the first film had. It grossed almost $9 million in its first weekend and nearly $45 million overall.

It was the success of this third film that truly cemented Freddy Krueger's status as an iconic figure in American pop culture. He—such as the goalie-masked zombie Jason Voorhees, the chainsaw-wielding cannibal Leatherface and the mute Michael Myers—was quickly supplanting older charac-ters such as Dracula, Frankenstein's Monster and the Wolfman as the bogeyman who embodied the idea of monstrous evil in the mass consciousness, and like all bogeymen he was embraced by kids, both teenaged and younger, who have long been fascinated by these evil creatures. New Line was quick to capitalize on the popularity of their trademarked character and happily licensed his image to almost anyone who would meet their price.

The results were Freddy games, candy, masks and dolls, as well as plastic replicas of his famous clawed glove and a record album called "Freddy's Greatest Hits" that featured Robert Englund chortling over tracks such as "All I Have to Do Is Dream" and "Down in the Boiler Room" sung by the Elm Street Singers. Thanks mostly to the money brought in by Freddy and his films, New Line was quickly growing as a

"Freddy's Greatest Hits" wasn't the only album to immortalize Freddy Krueger in song (it's just the worst). As well as the ode to the bastard son of a 100 maniacs by The Fat Boys called "Are You Ready For Freddy?" that appeared on the soundtrack of the fourth film, there was also the first track off of the wildly popular 1990 album "He's the DJ, I'm the Rapper" by DJ Jazzy Jeff and the Fresh Prince. The song's entitled "Nightmare On My Street" and it's a typically lighthearted rap single from the duo who mastered the form. Unlike The Fat Boys tune, though, their song wasn't written specifically to appear on a *Nightmare* soundtrack; they just really liked Freddy and wanted to write a song about him. Robert Englund ended up appearing as Freddy in the videos for both songs. For my money though, neither track holds a candle to *the best* single ever written as an ode to a movie maniac, "He's Back (The Man Behind the Mask)," a tribute to Jason Voorhees that Alice Cooper wrote for *Friday the 13th Part 6: Jason Lives* (1996).

force in Hollywood. The company moved out of New York and into Los Angeles and started making bigger and more expensive films.

For the next film in the series, *A Nightmare On Elm Street 4: The Dream Master* (1988), an up-and-coming director from Finland named Renny Harlin was hired to direct the film.[29] Seven screenwriters worked on the script,[30] and it showed on screen. The plot essentially consisted of only a few imaginative set pieces in which Freddy killed his victims, almost always with a punch line at the end. It was in this film that the character started his slide from an occasionally witty serial killer into what Wes Craven himself referred to as the "Henny Youngman of horror movies."[31] Still, the film took in nearly $50 million at the box office, making it the most successful film in the series.[32] But the film was also the most expensive in the series, costing $13 million to produce, four times the cost of the third film and over six times the cost of the first film.

---

29 His previous credits included the jail-based horror movie *Prison* (1988) and one of the most offensively jingoistic movies of the 1980s, *Born American* (1986). Following *Nightmare 4* he went on to direct several megabudget action movies, including the fun *The Long Kiss Goodnight* (1996) and the megabomb *Cutthroat Island* (1995), both of which starred his then-wife Geena Davis.

30 Novelist William Kotzwinkle (*Doctor Rat* and *The Bear Went Over the Mountain*) and Brian Helgeland (*L.A. Confidential* (1997) and *A Knight's Tale* (2001)) each received a story credit, while the screenplay credit went to Helgeland and Scott Pierce. Pierce was a pseudonym shared by the other five people who worked on the screenplay. They were Jim and Ken Wheat (*The Fly II* (1989) and *Pitch Black* (2000)), Michael De Luca (who soon became an executive at New Line), Renny Harlin, and Rachel Talalay (who would go on to direct the sixth film in the *Nightmare* series).

31 A quote that apparently so offended the elderly comedian that he threatened to sue Craven when he saw it in print.

32 That is until the tremendous success of *Freddy Vs. Jason* (2003), but we're getting ahead of ourselves aren't we?

Instead of continuing in that direction, the fifth film, *A Nightmare On Elm Street: The Dream Child*[33] (1989), was produced for half as much, which was prudent since it only took in $22 million. The tide had turned and audiences were seemingly growing disenchanted with the Freddy character. He was becoming too ubiquitous, having starred on a syndicated TV show called *Freddy's Nightmares* the year before. His overexposure, along with the new film's overreliance on bad jokes, had diminished Freddy's terrifying persona to the point that he was no longer frightening. He was now as scary and omnipresent as Count Chocula or Casper, the Friendly Ghost. Sensing this, Robert Shaye and his executives made the decision to kill him off for good.[34]

Not wanting to let the character who had built their company go out with a whimper, New Line decided that Part 6 needed a gimmick worthy of the old-school cinematic showmen. There had been a few 3D films released in the early 1980s,[35] but it had almost been a decade since then, so New Line felt the time was right to film parts of it in 3D and bring back the old cardboard glasses. Regardless of this—more annoying than amusing—novelty factor, the film was a creative, if not financial disappointment. *Freddy's Dead: The Final Nightmare* (1991) eventually grossed over $31 million—$9 million more than Part 5, a jump in the box office that had the company soon regretting their decision to kill off their most popular character.

---

33 Directed by Stephen Hopkins, who would later make *Predator 2* (1990) and *The Ghost and the Darkness* (1996).

34 A decision somewhat hampered by the fact that a) he was already dead and b) no one believed for a second that they would never bring him back again.

35 Most notably *Friday the 13th: Part 3* (1982) and *Jaws 3-D* (1983).

Craven, meanwhile, had survived the failure of *Deadly Friend* and followed it with *The Serpent and the Rainbow* (1988), a film[36] about the Haitian practice of voodoo. The film did well critically, but failed to make much money at the box office. His next film, *Shocker* (1989), was a blatant attempt to recreate the success of the *Nightmare* series and start a new horror franchise. It didn't work. *The People Under the Stairs* (1991), on the other hand, did. Easily one of the most interesting films of Craven's career, it's essentially an R-rated, urban fairy tale filled with emasculated cannibals and deviant sexuality that works as Craven's savage critique of Ronald Reagan's America, while also managing to be both extremely creepy and funny as hell.

Deeply unsatisfied with how New Line handled his most famous character, Craven became intrigued with an idea for a film that would strip away all of the campiness in the subsequent sequels and make Freddy the terrifying monster that he once was, as in the first *Nightmare*. When he pitched the idea to New Line, the company was flush with the feeling of success. In 1993 the company, thanks mostly to the steady income of the *Nightmare* franchise, was bought by billionaire cable mogul Ted Turner for $5.5 million and had recently established Fine Line as a niche studio devoted to releasing more serious art films. Robert Shaye and his executives were now open to new ideas and liked the idea of taking the character into a new direction. Craven's idea also solved a nagging problem for the company. They had marketed *Freddy's Dead* as being the last film in the *Nightmare* series, but it had done so well that it just made financial sense to follow it with

36 Based on the book by author Wade Davis.

a sequel. This was no longer an issue, because Craven's screenplay was so innovative that it could not be confused for a conventional sequel. It was a whole new beginning.

Craven's script for *A Nightmare On Elm Street Part 7: The Real Story* (the working title) didn't take place on Elm Street. It took place in Hollywood, and its main character was a 30-year-old mother/actress named Heather Langenkamp, whose greatest claim to fame was playing the character of Nancy Thompson in Wes Craven's *A Nightmare On Elm Street*. Strange things start happening to Heather and her young son, Dylan, not long after the last Freddy movie is made. She soon discovers that these unsettling incidents are happening to everyone involved with the franchise, including her costars John Saxon and Robert Englund, as well as Wes Craven and producers Robert Shaye and Sara Risher, who all play themselves in the film. It is Craven who figures out what is happening to all of them. The character of Freddy, he explains to Heather, was based on an ancient and powerful force of evil whose only weakness was its own vanity. It wanted to be feared by everyone, so it spared all those who told others of its existence. As long as stories were told about the evil, it would not rise, but as soon as the stories stopped it would return. The last *Nightmare* has been made, so the evil has started tormenting the men and women responsible for the series, and it will not stop until another sequel is made.[37]

Two years before *Scream*, Craven wrote and directed the first truly great postmodern horror film. *New Nightmare*

---

37 Perhaps the most effective moment in the whole film is the one where Craven explains to Heather his theory and tells her that he is working on the screenplay for the sequel at that moment. This is followed by a shot of his computer monitor, on which we can see the dialogue that he and Heather have just exchanged.

(1994)[38] did exactly what he wanted it to do with his rein-vented Freddy Krueger, and he did it in the most unique and interesting way possible. Unfortunately, it wasn't what the fans wanted. *New Nightmare* made even less than Part 5, ensuring that there would be no *Newer Nightmare*, or any Freddy films for a long while.

This chapter would likely have ended here, were it not for a little in-joke thrown in at the end of *Jason Goes to Hell: The Final Friday* (1993).[39] New Line had bought the rights to the Jason Voorhees character from Paramount after *Friday the 13th Part VIII: Jason Takes Manhattan* (1989) and attempted to reinvent him with this film. As a treat for hor-ror movie fans, the film ended with a shot of Freddy's famous steel-clawed glove reaching out of the ground and pulling Jason's famous hockey mask down underneath the soil, presumably to hell. This quick shot, which lasted only for a few seconds, instantly fueled speculation among geeks that these two horror icons would soon be appearing together on-screen. New Line soon took heed of this speculation and started developing a project with the rather obvious title of *Freddy Vs. Jason*, but it proved to be an idea that needed some time to percolate. Many different scripts were written and abandoned, some serious and many absurd,[40] until the two

---

38 In commentaries, Craven frequently refers to it as *Part 7*, but I think New Line was correct to try to establish it as something new and different.

39 Note that this was the *second* film featuring the character of Jason Voorhees to include the world "final" in its title. The fourth film in the *Friday the 13th* series having been sub-titled *The Final Chapter*. Note also that this second "final" film was also followed by more films in the series.

40 In one script, the third act consisted of Freddy and Jason fighting in a boxing match ref-ereed by Hitler. That's not a joke.

monsters met on-screen in 2003. The movie, directed by Ronny Yu,[41] was certainly entertaining, if only a little disappointing, considering the decade-long buildup. Still, it earned over $82 million at the box office, ensuring that it will not be the last time that these two fiends get together.

Freddy wasn't the only one who made a comeback following the failure of *New Nightmare*. In 1996,[42] Craven directed a smart satire of slasher movies called *Scream*[43] and ended up with the biggest hit of his career. The film starred several of Hollywood's hottest young actors, many of whom took parts in the film just for the chance to work with the famous master of horror. In interviews they talked about having grown up with his films and how they now wanted to be a part of them.

It is official, Wes Craven is now an institution. Given the dramatic ups and downs of his tumultuous career, it can be surmised that when people talk about his legacy, they aren't referring to *Deadly Blessing, The Hills Have Eyes II, Deadly Friend* or *Shocker*, they are talking about *A Nightmare On Elm Street*. Even after the enormous success of the *Scream* trilogy,[44] *A Nightmare On Elm Street* and the character of

---

41 Whose previous horror efforts include *The Bride With White Hair* (1993) and *Bride of Chucky* (1998).

42 A year earlier, Craven made the horror comedy *Vampire in Brooklyn* (1995) starring Eddie Murphy as a suave Blacula clone. It's the kind of movie that almost isn't worthy of its own footnote.

43 Craven included not one but two nods to the *Nightmare* series in *Scream*. One was a line that appeared in Kevin Williamson's script in which one of the characters mentions the series, noting that "The first one was good, but the rest of them sucked." And in one shot that delighted every horror movie fan who saw it, Craven himself can be seen as the high school janitor, dressed in Freddy's famous sweater and fedora.

44 *Scream 2* came in 1997 and *Scream 3* was released in 2000.

And speaking of remembering.... Remember when this chapter began all those pages ago and I mentioned how Miramax was forced to halt development on two Peter Jackson films based on J.R.R. Tolkein's *Lord of the Rings*? Well, when they did, Jackson took what he had and pitched it to Robert Shaye at New Line. It was Shaye who suggested that they make three films instead of two, and the rest is movie history. Given how important the *Nightmare* series was in the early years of New Line's development as a company, it is possible to suggest that were it not for Freddy Krueger, the artistically and financially successful Tolkein trilogy might never have been made.

Freddy Krueger remains Wes Craven's most important and influential contribution to the cinematic arts. It is the film for which he will always be remembered.

And what will happen to Freddy? Who knows? He's beaten the odds by lasting this long that's for sure. And, you know, as sellouts go, you have to admit, that old demon is pretty entertaining.

Also Look For

The entire *Nightmare* series is available on DVD, as is *Freddy Vs. Jason*. Copies of "Freddy's Greatest Hits," on the other hand, are fairly hard to come by. Consider yourself blessed.

It's So Good to Be Bad

The Good

Sure, everyone can name the really famous bad guys such as Freddy Krueger, Jason Voorhees and *The Texas Chainsaw Massacre*'s Leatherface, but here are five baddies who are just as entertainingly evil as those three, but who haven't earned even half as much recognition.

1) Belial Bradley (puppet/animated) - *Basket Case* (1982): For a little guy who can literally be kept in a small wicker basket, Belial sure managed to get into a lot of trouble, but it's easy to understand his rage and anger when you consider what he went through as a kid. He and his brother Duane were born as Siamese twins, but his parents never treated him like a son, considering him instead to be a diseased, living tumor growing out of their other, normal, child. Eventually, the parents hired three veterinarians to remove Belial from Duane and he was unceremoniously dumped into the garbage when they were done. Duane managed to save his brother, and the two of them have been together ever since, taking vengeance on anyone who would dare to even think of treating them as freaks.

2) Dr. Anton Phibes (Vincent Price) - *The Abominable Dr. Phibes* (1971): His face destroyed in a car accident and now only able to speak through a machine, Dr. Phibes cheated death so he could claim his revenge on the nine doctors who failed to save the life of his beloved wife, Victoria. Aided by a mysterious and beautiful young woman named Vulnavia, he kills them one by one using Moses' plagues on Egypt as his murderous theme. Though he could not complete his final revenge before he returned to the grave to be with his beloved wife, he would rise again...

3) Sister Hyde (Martine Beswick) - *Dr. Jekyll and Sister Hyde* (1971): What many people aren't aware of is that Jack the Ripper wasn't a Jack at all, he was a Jill instead. It all started when a young scientist named Dr. Henry Jekyll made the silly mistake of testing out his new experimental serum on himself. This strange potion proved to have the strangest of all side-effects; it transformed Dr. Jekyll into his feminine alter-ego, a gorgeous but deadly young woman who called herself Sister Hyde. Needing the serum to ensure her own continued existence, this twisted sister was forced to find a steady supply of dead bodies in order to obtain the elixir's key ingredient. Not burdened with her male counterpart's morality, she had no problem procuring these bodies herself. She went to White Chapel and lured a series of desperate prostitutes to an early grave, and was stopped only when her bloody trail led the police to the doomed, but innocent Dr. Jekyll.

4) Julie Walker (Melinda Clarke) - *Return of the Living Dead III* (1993): Julie was not so much a villain as an unwilling victim of her own resurrection. When she died from a broken neck after a motorcycle accident, her boyfriend Curt decided to take her back to the army base where his father worked and exposed her to the same chemicals that he had once seen bring a dead man back to life. Living again, Julie felt a pain she could not describe. At first she fought against it by cutting herself and piercing her flesh with needles, transforming herself into the ultimate alternative Goth girl, but soon this was not enough and she could no longer fight off her urge to consume fresh, living brains and she became the coolest and sexiest zombie cannibal of all time.

5) The Collector (Billy Zane) - *Tales From the Crypt Presents Demon Knight* (1995): Resembling that rich jerk who was so mean to Leonardo DiCaprio in *Titanic* (1997), The Collector is just one of a group of demons who have spent the past 2,000 years in search of the key they need to open up the gates of Hell. During that time, the key has been kept safe by another group, known as the Demon Knights who have, one by one, done their best to keep the demons from taking over the world. One quiet night in a small-town, rundown hotel, The Collector catches up with the latest Demon Knight and comes very, very close to ending the world, and he does it all with a sly, easy grin and an unwillingness to lose his wicked sense of humor.

The Not-So-Good

But then again, some scary movie villains don't really deserve any recognition at all. Whether it was because they tried too hard, not hard enough, or were just too flawed in their conception, these baddies are best left overlooked.

1) Ben Willis (Muse Watson) - *I Know What You Did Last Summer* **(1997):** Imagine that you were a guy who had been run over by a bunch of young kids driving around in an expensive sports car, and instead of calling an ambulance or the police, they decide to dump your still-living body into the ocean, but you manage to survive and begin to hunt and kill the kids, one by one, a year later. Wanting to frighten them as much as you can, you decide to stalk them wearing the most fearsome-looking outfit you can think of. Of all the possible choices you have, would you ever think of dressing like a fisherman? Well, you aren't Ben Willis and you probably would have made a much better villain than he did.

2) Horace Pinker (Mitch Pileggi) - *Shocker* **(1989):** Horace Pinker is what you get when you try to create a character who can carry a horror movie franchise and fail. Wes Craven tried to create another Freddy Krueger with this story of a serial killer who is turned into an unstoppable supernatural force after his death in the electric chair. The problem is that Freddy had style, and Horace is just the bald guy from *The X-Files* in an orange prison jumpsuit. He isn't frightening, and the only time he's funny is when he isn't trying to be, like when he possesses a young blonde moppet and has her drive a bulldozer towards the movie's hero. It isn't any surprise then that none of the planned sequels were ever made.

3) The Leprechaun (Warwick Davis) - *Leprechaun* **(1993):** One of the great mysteries of the horror genre is how a film as badly misconceived as *Leprechaun* could prove successful enough for a sequel, but successful enough to allow for, as of this writing, *five* sequels in the continuing story of this murderous member of the little people. Since he is neither frightening nor funny, I know of no one who eagerly anticipates his next adventure, yet he keeps appearing in our video stores every two years or so. Why? If someone out there knows the answer, I would truly appreciate it.

4) Dr. Evan Rendell (Larry Drake) - *Dr. Giggles* **(1992):** He's a doctor, y'see, but he's really crazy, so he kills people and giggles while he does it. People got paid for creating him. Seriously. Makes you think...

5) Trickster (T. Ryder Smith) - *Brainscan* **(1994):** He's just like Freddy, only he sucks! The most amazing thing about this incredibly annoying and unimaginative character is that he was created by Andrew Kevin Walker, the writer who would go on to write the brilliant *Seven* (1995) and *Sleepy Hollow* (1999), as well make significant contributions to David Fincher's masterpiece *Fight Club* (1999). This proves once again that sometimes even the best of us don't always get it right.

5
A Sad Tale of Love and Goo

The Fly

They met at a party.
He told her he was going to change the world
and she didn't believe him,
so he took her back to his place to prove it.
There he showed her how he could take a solid object,
disintegrate it, move it across space
and then reassemble it in another spot.

She was shocked.
He had told her the truth.
He was working on something that could change the world.
She tried to write about it,
but he stopped her and convinced her to wait until his experiments
were finished
and he could teleport living tissue,
which had thus far proved to be a tough nut to crack.
She agreed and started observing him as he worked.

Seeing him in his element, she grew attracted to him
and this attraction turned into love.
He loved her back and grew jealous one night
when she went away to deal with the problems of a past relationship.

Drunk on celebratory wine,
he decided to complete his final experiment
by teleporting himself across the room.

This last experiment seemed to be a success,
but there was one tiny little problem.

A fly had joined him in his telepod
and its genes fused together with his at the molecular level.

At first he felt stronger and more alive than he ever had before,
but gradually he realized that he was changing
into something that could no longer be considered human.

His relationship with the girl would never be the same...

The Evil Genius

I can be a sucker for a romantic story, believe it or not.
— David Cronenberg, *Cronenberg On Cronenberg*

I would have been around the age of eight the first time I heard the name David Cronenberg. It was 1983 and our local cable company had just started Pay TV, where people had the option of paying a few dollars extra each month for stations that showed uncensored movies 24 hours a day.[1] To promote this new venture, the cable company devoted time on its public access channel to previews for the films that were then airing on the new stations. A budding cineast even at that early age, I would frequently sit down and enjoy these previews whenever a quick turn of the dial[2] proved that there was nothing else on the tube worth watching. Interestingly, there was no thematic order to the collections of clips, thus a preview for the animated fantasy *The Last Unicorn* (1982) could easily be followed by a clip for the first Rambo movie, *First Blood* (1982), depending on what films the channels were showing that month. This made for a slightly tense— but very exciting—viewing experience, as you had no idea what you would see next. I don't recall what preview aired before the one that forever burned the name Cronenberg into my psyche, but—no matter what it was—it *had* to be tame by comparison.

---

1 I feel so incredibly old when I think back to those days and realize that *with* cable, a non-Pay TV subscriber was limited to 13 channels.

2 Dials! Man, we had it bad back then.

The image lingered with me for years after I saw it just that one time.[3] It consisted of a television set whose screen was filled by a pair of luscious red lips. A man, kneeling in front of the TV, moved towards it and the lips caused the screen to expand forward, as if the screen wasn't a screen but instead a very real mouth. The man touched the lips and then—to my horror—pressed his head against them. What scared me most wasn't the moment's intensely aberrant sexuality (I mean, I was only eight at the time), but my utter fear that the lips would open up and reveal a set of gleaming white teeth and chomp down on the crazy man's neck and devour his head. But before this nightmare could come true, the image was replaced with the film's title, *Videodrome* (1983), which an off-screen voice announced to me was "A David Cronenberg Film." From that moment on I knew that whoever Cronenberg was, he had to be *evil*.[4]

Later on I would learn that this was not the first time I had encountered a truly "Cronenbergian" moment. My first exposure to his madness was the ad campaign for his earlier film *Scanners* (1981), which consisted of various shots of people on the verge of exploding from some mysterious psychic force. According to the word around school, that movie contained a scene where a man's head—in the immortal words of SCTV's "Prairie Film Report"—"blew up *real*

---

3 I stopped watching the preview show immediately after, and thereafter made every effort to avoid the channel it aired on.

4 I would later learn that this was not a unique reaction when I read that no less a cinematic authority than Martin Scorsese expressed shock when he met Cronenberg for the first time. He was expecting to meet a depraved maniac, but instead he was introduced to a handsome, urbane gentleman who most resembled an English professor. Given much of the content of Cronenberg's films, it's an honest mistake to make.

good."[5] And three years after I was traumatized by *Videodrome's* twisted imagery, I would hear the name Cronenberg again as I listened to my peers gleefully relate the goriest aspects of his latest assault on polite society, *The Fly* (1986).

"There's this scene where the doctor guy tries to teleport a monkey, but it doesn't work and it turns the monkey[6] inside out!"

"So, he's looking in the mirror and his ear falls off!"

"He pulls off his fingernail and then he squeezes his finger and all of this pus comes out!"

"He vomits acid on a guy's hand and foot and they both melt!"

"This lady gives birth to a great big maggot!"

"—And then she grabs at his face and his jaw comes off right in her hand!"

Needless to say, hearing these not-so-delightful (and completely out of context) tidbits was definitely more than enough to support my previously held contention that this Cronenberg guy was the sickest man on the planet. And so, it should come as no surprise to you that of all of the films that I didn't yet have the stomach to sit through, his were the ones I was dying to see the most.

But as much as I wanted to see his films, I waited a long time before I felt sufficiently brave enough to face them. A part of me was still tormented by that brief clip I had seen

---

5 Thanks to kids with older siblings (or neglectful parents), tales of disgusting scenes of cinematic mayhem were told as if they were a strange folklore from a far-off land. Wanting to join in, but not having the stomach or the opportunities to witness such gruesome sights, I was prone to making up scenes based on the information I gleaned from the poster. I think this was my first step towards becoming a writer.

6 It's actually a baboon in the film, but most sixth-graders at that time failed to note the distinction.

from *Videodrome*, so I decided to choose another film as my premier Cronenbergian experience. In the end I chose *The Fly* to serve that role, largely for the very important reason that Geena Davis was in it and I had been in love with her ever since she played an incompetent nanny/housekeeper on a *Family Ties* episode a few years earlier.

Before I describe to you what I saw, I want to explain to you what it is that truly distinguishes a film fanatic from someone who merely enjoys a good movie. It's a moment. It's a moment every serious film buff has experienced and one that we spend the rest of our lives trying to relive. It is the moment when a film—it doesn't matter which one[7]—causes your mind to soar and touches you so powerfully it makes you want to devote your whole life to it. It is the moment when you realize that movies are about the glory of our dreams, not just entertainment.

When I saw David Cronenberg's *The Fly* for the first time, I experienced one of these rare and highly treasured moments. It was the film that transformed me from a young kid curious about horror movies into a devoted fanatic, and not for the reasons that you think. What shocked me most about the film was not its gooey violence or its graphic imagery, but how much it made me care. When the film was over, there were tears in my eyes. I am a sucker for a good tearjerker and have often been moved to tears by both good and bad movies alike, but never had I ever considered the possibility that a horror movie could have such an effect on me. I could not believe that a film that contained all the horrific

---

7 Although *Citizen Kane* (1941) and *Star Wars* (1977) both seem to be very popular choices.

moments described above could do more than simply frighten and disgust. It was the film that showed me that David Cronenberg wasn't evil, he was—as far as the word could ever be applied to a man who makes movies—a *genius.* An evil genius, maybe, but a genius nonetheless.

And what was it in *The Fly* that moved me as much as it did? I realized that I was watching a tragic love story that would not have been possible in any other genre. With *The Fly,* Cronenberg took the Hollywood cliché of the transformative powers of love and made it literal, and by doing so showed it to be the fairy tale fantasy it really is.[8] It stunned me to realize that by employing a fantastic narrative, a filmmaker could make a more honest and realistic film than someone working with a straight drama or comedy. It taught me that a horror movie could get away with themes and ideas that a more mainstream film would never be able to touch. And the fact that so many other people are blind to these hidden subtexts only make them that much more appealing.

In other films, love would be what saves the main character, Seth Brundle, but in Cronenberg's movie it is what dooms him. The reason he is transformed into the titular monster is not because a housefly joined him in his telepod that fateful night, but because his jealously towards his girlfriend meeting with her ex caused him to get drunk and decide to get in the telepod in the first place.

---

8 Call me crazy, but I consider *The Fly* to be a much more emotionally realistic film than, say, *Pretty Woman* (1990), where we're meant to feel happy that the streetwalker played by Julia Roberts (who is as convincing as a working girl as Dustin Hoffman would be playing Muhammad Ali) is able to get off the street and become the girlfriend of wealthy Richard Gere.

At first, his transformation is a blessing. He's a stronger, better man than he ever has been before, but he cannot stop changing into a fly, and he very soon ceases to be the man that his girlfriend fell in love with. He attempts to force her to stay with him forever, but she refuses and, in the end, he becomes so monstrous that he urges her to permanently end his suffering. Aside from the main character turning into a great big bug, Cronenberg made a film that examines how a relationship goes terribly wrong. It's the classic case of the guy who gets the girl of his dreams and screws it all up because his self-doubt makes him feel that he doesn't really deserve her. As he works so hard to become the guy he thinks she wants, she becomes more alienated because he's no longer the guy she used to know, and the relationship gradually crumbles.

(Plus the scene where his jaw comes off is totally kick-ass!)

And I did eventually sit down and watch *Videodrome*, and as twisted as it was, it didn't even come close to being as terrifying as my own imagination had imagined it would be when I was eight. Now that was *evil*.

How It Happened

David Cronenberg is that rarest of cinematic creatures, a genuine auteur. He is one of the only directors working today who actually deserves that title, because for almost 30 years now he has been making films so completely his own that the only word that adequately describes them is *Cronenbergesque*. His vision has proved so unique that it created an entirely new horror movie genre, one in which the monsters that attacked us weren't murderous psychos, mind-less aliens or supernatural creatures of the night, but our own minds and bodies. The battle between good and evil is straightforward compared to the complexities that rage inside ourselves.

Born in 1943 in the Canadian city of Toronto, Ontario, to intellectually minded middle-class parents, he grew up with a mutual fascination for science and literature. "I wrote my first novel when I was 10 years old," he admitted to Chris Rodley, the editor of the book-long interview entitled *Cronenberg On Cronenberg.* "It was three pages long." As for his interest in science, he "...was fascinated by the way people dig around to discover how things work, and the way they codify and organize that knowledge." Later on in his life, both of these interests would have a major impact on the kind of films he would make.

When he went to the University of Toronto, he decided to pursue a degree in science, believing that a person couldn't be taught to be a writer, but they could be taught how to be a scientist. When he realized that he was spending all of his time "...at the arts end of the campus," he dropped out of his science courses a year later and enrolled in the university's English program. Never a big fan of movies, Cronenberg was stunned when—not long after he switched majors—he saw a very low-budget film entitled *Winter Kept Us Warm,* which was made by a fellow student named David Secter. Secter's little movie was filmed around the university and was cast with several of Cronenberg's friends, and the effect of seeing people and locations he knew so well on screen made him believe for the first time that "...film [was] something I could do, something I had access to."

Cronenberg's ignorance of film history and previous indifference to the medium would later prove to be a blessing rather than a curse. One of the major reasons his films seemed so different and unique when they first came out was because they were not inspired by anything that came before them. Cronenberg was a cinematic blank slate and he felt no need to follow any of moviemaking's established rules.

Inspired by Secter's movie, Cronenberg decided to make his own films. He started with two surreal shorts called *Transfer* (1966) and *From the Drain* (1967), and followed them up with two much more ambitious projects, the nearly feature-length *Stereo* (1969) and *Crimes of the Future* (1970). Both of these films were obviously the product of an overly self-indulgent 20-something filmmaker, but they contained themes and motifs that would later appear in his more professional efforts, including *The Fly*. Cronenberg set both films in clinics dedicated to experimental science (The Canadian Academy For Erotic Inquiry in *Stereo* and The House of Skin in *Crimes of the Future*). Science and its effect on society would later serve as a major theme in his work.[9]

After making several more short films, Cronenberg got the opportunity to make his feature-length script *Orgy of the Blood Parasites* into his first mainstream film. The story of a doctor who creates a parasite that causes people to lose all of their inhibitions and act out their basest animal desires, the film—retitled *Shivers*[10]—ignited a flood of controversy in

---

9 Later examples of similar scientific institutions include the Keloid Clinic in *Rabid* (1977), the Somafree Institute in *The Brood* (1979), Consec in *Scanners,* the O'Blivion Centre in *Videodrome*, Bartok Industries in *The Fly* and the Mantle Clinic in *Dead Ringers* (1988).

10 It would also end up being released as *They Came From Within* and *The Parasite Murders*.

Cronenberg's home country when it was released there in 1975. Many people were appalled that such a violent and unsettling film had been made with money from the Canadian government's film fund,[11] but not all of the reaction to the film was negative. Critics and fans all over the world recognized that Cronenberg's debut was unlike anything they had ever seen and represented a new direction in the world of horror movies.

Two years later Cronenberg followed up his first success with a film called *Rabid* (1977). The story of a young woman who is transformed into a living vampire after receiving experimental surgery following a motorcycle accident, the film's plot can easily be interpreted as an analogy for the effect a virulent sexually transmitted disease could have on society. Rose, the film's doomed protagonist, is able to lure in her victims thanks to her overt sexuality, and once she has fed from them, they too are infected. By the film's end, nearly all of Montreal is infected, and police and military crews are patroling the streets and disposing of the dead bodies. The film's obvious analogy was strengthened when the film's producers[12] cast the porn film actress Marilyn Chambers as the main character Rose.[13] Chambers' performance turned out to be very good, and it became one of the film's strongest assets. In his DVD commentary for the film, Cronenberg

---

11 Willfully ignoring that it was the first film produced by the fund to turn a profit.

12 One of whom was Ivan Reitman, the future director of *Ghostbusters* (1984), *Twins* (1988) and *Dave* (1993).

13 Cronenberg's choice had been Sissy Spacek, who had made a name for herself in Terrance Malick's *Badlands* (1973). The film's producers were worried about her accent and didn't think she was right to play the lead in a horror movie, but when *Carrie* came out as *Rabid* was filming, they admitted they might have been wrong.

admits to not understanding why her performance didn't lead her on to a more mainstream career.

After *Rabid* came *Fast Company* (1979), a film that was almost completely forgotten by fans until its recent release on DVD. The reason for its absence in the minds of movie-goers has less to do with its quality as it does with the fact that it bears no resemblance to any of his other movies. It's a car-racing picture, and as car-racing pictures go, it's okay, but there is nothing about the film to distinguish it from a hundred other low-budget exploitation movies made during that period.[14]

That same year saw the release of a much more personal film for Cronenberg, *The Brood* (1979). For years now, Cronenberg has joked that the film was his version of the hit movie *Kramer Vs. Kramer* (1979), but the truth is that he was very much inspired to make the film after a painful custody battle over his daughter with his first wife. It tells the story of Frank Carveth, whose disturbed wife Nola has been commit-ted to an institute run by Dr. Hal Raglan, the creator of a treatment that teaches his patients to transform their mental illnesses—such as extreme cases of anger and depression—into physical illnesses—such as cancer—that can be more easily cured. Frank is worried that Nola has abused their young daughter and will continue to do so once she is released from the clinic. His fears grow worse when bruises begin appearing on his daughter and Nola's parents are murdered. He eventually discovers that due to Dr. Raglan's treatment, Nola has transformed her anger into mutant children—her brood—that grow out of her skin and then go

---

14 Nothing except the personal note that it was filmed in my hometown of Edmonton, Alberta.

on to attack whoever has caused the anger to exist in the first place. The film's central conceit that rage, if improperly treated, can easily lead to physical violence is a common one, but it has seldom been explored as creatively as it is here.

A year later Cronenberg made *Scanners*, a fairly routine science-fiction action movie best remembered for the scene where Canadian character actor Louis Del Grande's head explodes.[15] He then went way out the mainstream with 1983's *Videodrome*, a film which deliberately plays with the audience's notions of straightforward linear narrative as it descends into a world where it becomes impossible to tell the difference between reality and fantasy—a strategy he would again explore in 1999's *eXistenZ*. That same year he made *The Dead Zone* (1983), an adaptation of Stephen King's best-selling book that marked the first time he directed a film with a finished script he did not contribute to. The result was one of the best of the many King adaptations released during that period, thanks mostly to a haunting performance by Christopher Walken as Johnny Smith, a man gifted with psychic abilities he'd rather not have.

After the success of *The Dead Zone*, Cronenberg was considered a bankable director in Hollywood and—as a result—was offered several projects that would later become hit movies, including *Beverly Hills Cop* (1984), *Witness* (1985) and *Flashdance* (1983). He chose instead to pursue an adaptation of a Phillip K. Dick short story called "We Can Remember It for You Wholesale" that was being produced by Dino De Laurentiis. The title of the story had been changed

---

15 Cronenberg would have nothing to do with the various sequels that followed. A remake is also currently in development.

to *Total Recall* and the project had been around for years as various directors worked on its appealing premise of a world where people could have memories of adventures they never had transplanted into their minds. After a year working on the project, Cronenberg quit when it became clear to him that De Laurentiis wanted a more typical action movie instead of the project he envisioned.[16]

Having spent so much time on *Total Recall* without getting the film made, Cronenberg was eager to find a project he could start right away. Surprisingly, his best offer came from Mel Brooks, the director, writer and actor responsible for the low-comedy classics *The Producers* (1968), *Blazing Saddles* (1974) and *Young Frankenstein* (1974). Wanting to stretch himself beyond comedy, Brooks had formed a production company, Brooksfilms, so he could make films he normally wouldn't be associated with. Among the films the company would eventually make were the critical successes *The Elephant Man* (1980), *Frances* (1982), *My Favorite Year (1982)* and *84 Charing Cross Road* (1987), as well as more lamentable features such as *Fatso* (1980) and *Solarbabies* (1986). The company was eager to produce a new script by a screenwriter named Charles Edward Pogue[17] that was based on a famous monster movie from 1958 called *The Fly*,[18]

---

16 Cronenberg wanted to cast Richard Dreyfuss to play the role so it would force people to constantly question what was happening to him and whether or not it was real or a dream. De Laurentiis, leery of another big-budget adventure film after the failure of *Dune* (1984), eventually sold the rights to the story and the script, and the film was eventually made six years later by Paul Verhoeven, *Robocop* (1987) starring Arnold Schwarzenegger. As a result, the film's supposedly ambiguous ending never seems ambiguous at all.

17 Whose only other notable scary movie credit is his underrated script for 1986's *Psycho III*.

18 Which itself was based on a short story by George Langelaan and adapted for the screen by future *Shogun* author James Clavell.

which was about what happened when a scientist transformed himself into two different monstrous creatures after a disastrous experiment in teleportation. One of the creatures had the body of a man and the head of a fly, and the other one had the head of a man and the body of a fly.[19] This new version changed the story, so that instead of an instant transformation, the scientist first appears normal when he walks out of his invention and only gradually becomes the monster in stages as the movie progresses.

Cronenberg liked the script's premise more than the actual script, so once he agreed to do the movie, he essentially started from scratch and jettisoned the script's original characters, dialogue and ending. Not all of Pogue's ideas were thrown out however, as Cronenberg loved the scenes where the scientist's fingernails fell off and the fact that the transformation gave the character superhuman strength.

However, Cronenberg changed Pogue's family-man protagonist into a socially inept, yet still strangely attractive, loner named Seth Brundle who worked by himself and had no friends or family. He intended to a create a character who has changed, even before he puts himself through the machine that will eventually turn him into a monster. To that end he also created the role of a female journalist named Veronica Quaife, who manages to charm Brundle out of his shell and give him his very first taste of romantic love. By doing this Cronenberg took what could have been a standard horror movie and instead transformed it into a tragic romance. One is almost tempted to think of the film as the

---

19 The original film's most famous moment occurs when the tiny flyman gets caught in a spider's web and calls out *"Help me!"* in a pitiful and high-pitched voice, until his brother (played by Vincent Price) comes upon him and mercifully smashes him with a rock.

scary movie version of *Love Story* (1970), but to do so would serve *The Fly* a disservice, since it lacks the manipulative sentiment that pervades in Arthur Hiller's tearjerker.

Budgeted at $10 million, the film—like almost all of Cronenberg's movies—was shot in his hometown of Toronto. The story he was telling was intimate and had a very small cast for what would have been a mid-budget Hollywood film at the time, so it was important that the right actors be chosen. For the character of Seth, Jeff Goldblum was an actor who could convincingly portray the character as a misfit while still remaining attractive enough that the audience could believe that a beautiful and intelligent woman such as Veronica would want to have a relationship with him. For the part of Veronica, Cronenberg wanted an actress whose screen presence matched Goldblum. He didn't have to look far, since Goldblum's then-girlfriend, Geena Davis, had the same kind of indescribable vibe as her

This wasn't the first time that Jeff Goldblum and Geena Davis worked together, but considering how badly their first film turned out, it's a minor miracle that they were allowed to ever appear together on-screen again. The film was 1985's *Transylvania 6-5000* and in it Goldblum played an American reporter sent to Transylvania to investigate reports of the return of Frankenstein's monster. Davis appears as a deranged young woman who spends the entire film in a sexy, low-cut vampiress outfit (the sight of which—it must be admitted—*almost* makes the movie worth watching), in which she tries to seduce Ed Begley Jr. The almost shockingly unfunny comedy was written and directed by a bit-part actor named Rudy De Luca, who has—thankfully—never been allowed to direct another film since.

boyfriend, but was also one of the most beautiful actresses working at the time. For the part of Veronica's ex-boyfriend, Stathis Borans,[20] he hired a less well-known actor named John Getz, who had recently starred in the Coen Brother's first film, *Blood Simple* (1984).

Cronenberg chose Chris Walas to execute the film's many difficult creature effects. Walas worked on *Scanners*, as well as created the impressive alien makeup in *Enemy Mine* (1995). For his cinematographer, Cronenberg once again worked with Mark Irwin, who had previously filmed *The Dead Zone* and *Videodrome*. He also hired Carol Spier, who had worked on *The Dead Zone*, as his production designer, and she would go on to work on all his films from that point on. And he decided to take a chance on a first-time costume designer named Denise Cronenberg, who just happened to be his second wife. His frequent collaborator and fellow-Canadian Howard Shore[21] was hired to write the film's music, and with all of the major players in place the production went before the camera.

As was the case with several of his previous films, Cronenberg struggled to find the right ending to *The Fly*. In one version, Veronica married Stathis, and in another she gave birth to her and Seth's baby, but instead of being a disgusting maggot, the child is instead a beautiful butterfly creature. Test audiences hated Stathis and couldn't stomach the idea that Veronica would ever marry him, and they were still

---

20 One of Cronenberg's trademarks is that all of the characters he creates have strange and memorable names.

21 Who would later become the reigning king of epic scores after composing the music for both *Titanic* and the *Lord of the Rings* trilogy. He is also, at the time that this is being written, rumored to be working on a stage opera based on *The Fly*.

too overcome with grief from the tragic scene they had just witnessed to find any relief in the fact that the baby wasn't a monster after all. I think Cronenberg made the right choice in ending the film where he did—immediately after

For many people the dream sequence in which Veronica gives birth to the maggot is one of the most horrifying scenes in the entire film. For scary movie fans, though, the sequence is also memorable because it features David Cronenberg's only on-screen cameo in one of his own films. In it he plays the doctor who delivers and holds up Veronica and Seth's disgusting offspring. Even though he hasn't acted in any of his other films, Cronenberg has—since *The Fly*—had what can almost be described as a second career, appearing in other directors' films. Many of his roles have been brief cameos, such as the mobster he played in Gus Van Sant's *To Die For* (1995) or the lawyer who questions Hugh Grant near the end of Michael Apted's *Extreme Measures* (1996), but he has also been given larger and more important parts. In Clive Barker's *Nightbreed* (1990) he played a doctor/psychopathic serial killer, and in Canadian director Don McKeller's film *Last Night* (1998) he played an employee of an energy company who spends the day before the end of the world calling the company's customers and thanking them for their years of loyal patronage. Given that he has spent the last 20 years making films that play in art houses, it is refreshing to know that he is still willing to honor his genre-exploitation roots by making the occasional appearance in films *Blood & Donuts* (1995), *Resurrection* (1999) and *Jason X*. Most recently he has been spotted on the small screen portraying a bohemian scientist enlisted to help Jennifer Garner's character, Sidney Bristow, retrieve her memory in the action-filled TV show *Alias*.

the emotional climax—but I would have loved to have seen the birth of the butterfly child, if only because it would have spared us from the events that occurred in the film's extremely disappointing sequel.

The Aftermath

When it was released to theaters, *The Fly* proved to be that rarest of commodities, a gory horror film that was popular both with critics *and* audiences. It grossed over $7 million in its opening weekend and went on to make $40 million, which—for a horror movie in 1986—was more than enough for it to be considered a hit and for a sequel to be set in the works.

The film was also praised by critics as being both an exciting improvement over the original film it was based on, and as a fascinating allegory about the effect that illness and disease can have on a relationship. Despite all of the kudos the film received, the film's true merits were—like many other popular horror/fantasy films—ignored by the Oscars in favor of its technical achievements. Chris Walas won for Best Makeup for his work on Jeff Goldblum.

Being that he was the only person connected to the film to win an award for his work, it isn't that surprising that Walas was chosen to direct the film's sequel when Cronenberg declined. But one of the lessons of horror movie history is that very often films directed by great special effects artists tend to fail. Examples of this being true are Tom Savini's remake of *Night of the Living Dead* (1990), Stan Winston's *Pumpkinhead* (1989), *A Gnome Called Gnorm* (1992), Pitof's *Catwoman* (2004) and Screaming Mad George's *The Guyver*

(1991). Unfortunately, Chris Walas' work on *The Fly II* (1989) is no exception.

In truth, the sequel was hampered by the fact that none of the original actors except for John Getz were willing to return—and he played a character the audience loathed. Deciding to focus the sequel on Seth and Veronica's child, the filmmakers opened the film with a scene in which Veronica (played this time by Saffron Henderson)[22] dies giving birth. Thus the film begins with the death of the first film's most sympathetic character and goes downhill from there. Not wanting to have their protagonist be a child, or set the film in the future, it was decided that since the baby named Martin wasn't completely human, he could grow into adulthood in just a couple of scenes. Martin, played by Eric Stoltz, was a genius who—like his father—is destined to transform into a creature a lot less photogenic. Despite boasting great effects and a good performance from Stoltz, the sequel fails mostly because it lacks the pathos that made the first film so unique. Like many sequels, the film followed the original too closely, causing it to be much more predictable and uninvolving than it should be.

As for David Cronenberg, he followed the success of *The Fly* with what may very well be his masterpiece, *Dead Ringers* (1988). The film swept the Genie Awards[23] that year thanks largely to a brilliant performance by Jeremy Irons. Amazingly, Irons was ignored by the Oscars for his portrayal of identical twins Beverly and Elliot Mantle, but when he won the award

---

22 Who appears to have since had a busy career as a voice-over actress, featured mostly in English versions of Japanese cartoons.

23 Canada's equivalent of the Oscars.

"I'll hurt you if you stay." (Jeff Goldblum and Geena Davis in *The Fly*)

for Best Actor two years later for his performance as Claus Von Bulow in Barbet Schroeder's *Reversal of Fortune* (1990), he made sure to thank Cronenberg in his acceptance speech.

Starting with *Dead Ringers*, Cronenberg established himself as a filmmaker devoted to his own unique vision, resulting in a number of films that defy any conventional classification. This is especially true of his two literary adaptations, *Naked Lunch* (1991) and *Crash* (1996), both of which feature enough sex and violence to put any horror movie to shame, but in a way that makes it impossible to dismiss them as typical genre fare.[24] Since *The Fly* he has avoided working on studio films, preferring to work outside of the Hollywood system and financing his films through other means. But that's not to say he hasn't been tempted a few times to return to La La Land. In 2000 it was announced that he had been hired to remake the long-delayed sequel to Paul Verhoeven's 1992 sexual thriller *Basic Instinct*, which would mark the return of Sharon Stone as the murderous Catherine Tramell. It came as a shock to many of his fans to hear his name attached to such a potentially unremarkable project, but in interviews he said he signed on to make the film because he was really excited by the film's script. But the project became hopelessly derailed when Stone refused to accept the producer's decision to cast Benjamin Bratt as her costar and the film was never made.[25] At last word the script that had so impressed Cronenberg was rewritten to be made as a stand-alone project, and Cronenberg has moved on to other projects.

Also Look For

Anybody interested in the works of David Cronenberg should look for his book-long interview *Cronenberg On Cronenberg*, which was edited by Chris Rodley. For a far more in-depth look at his films, William Beard's 457-page tome *The Artist As Monster: The Cinema of David Cronenberg* is also worth finding. Unfortunately for fans of *The Fly*, the film is available only on a bare bones, two-sided DVD that includes the sequel. Given the film's continued popularity and revered status among scary movie fans, it definitely deserves to be reissued and updated with more features.

---

24 In his wonderful book *Profoundly Disturbing*, John Bloom—writing under his popular alias, Joe-Bob Briggs—points out that *Crash* may very well be the first film that begins with three extremely explicit sex scenes that are actually integral to the movie's plot.

25 It was somewhat ironic then that when Stone finally returned to the world of big-budget studio films after a long, illness-induced absence, it was in *Catwoman* (2004), a film whose main male role was played by—you guessed it—Benjamin Bratt.

Let's Try This One More Time

The Good

For some reason movie buffs tend to treat remakes the same way some children of divorce treat their new stepparents. They act as though embracing the remake means forsaking the original movie that they love, so to justify their knee-jerk rejection of it, they refuse to acknowledge the original's imperfections and see only the remake's faults. But, as David Cronenberg's version of *The Fly* proves, sometimes a remake is so good that not even the most stubborn defender of the original can deny his love. Here are five remakes that are better than their predecessors.

1) *Invasion of the Body Snatchers* (1978): Updating Don Siegel's classic adaptation of Jack Finney's novel, director Philip Kaufman and screenwriter W.D. Richter took the story of pod people replacing real humans out of the McCarthy era and into the New Age. Almost as effective as a parody of the twisted values of the Me Generation and the self-help movement as it is a horror movie, the film gets funnier and more frightening as it ages. In terms of pure emotional horror, few films mentioned in this book can compete with this film's final soul-crushing scene. Proving that a good story cannot die, this version of the film served as the basis for Abel Ferrara's 1993 remake, *Body Snatchers*, which is also worth checking out.

Zombies in the streets. (Extras from the remake of *Dawn of the Dead*)

2) *Dawn of the Dead* **(2004):** What I'm about to admit is as close to blasphemy as a scary movie fanatic can come, but I must confess—I think that Zack Snyder's remake of *Dawn of the Dead* is better and more enjoyable than the original film made by George Romero in 1978. People have told me that the original is a classic because of its wonderful satire and three-dimensional characters, but I have to take their word for it because *I have never been able to sit through the whole film!* It moves as slowly as its zombies and has put me to sleep every time I've tried to watch it. Snyder's film, on the other hand, is a thrilling ride filled with characters who may not be three-dimensional, but that are at least a lot of fun to watch.

3) *The Thing* (1982): It is only recently that John Carpenter's remake of 1951's *The Thing From Another World* has been getting the recognition it deserves. Released the same summer as *E.T.: The Extra-Terrestrial* (1982), audiences weren't looking for a story about a killer alien from outer space and the film flopped at the box office. Critically it was derided as being too violent and not nearly as good as the original. These days, however, people are able to see the film for the classic that it truly is. Even if you took away the film's infamous gore, it is still much more frightening and tense than the original, which today plays a bit too campy for its own good.

4) *The Ring* (2002): Gore Verbinski's remake of the 1998 Japanese film *Ringu* hasn't earned a lot of respect among fright film fans, but I think that has less to do with its success as a remake as it does with it being a success—period. Horror movie fans tend to be very suspicious of any scary movie that manages to capture the attention of mainstream filmgoers, and in this case I think they're doing the film a disservice. *The Ring* is an effectively chilling thriller with the kind of disturbing ending that lingers in the imagination for a good long while. Plus, that little girl is *crazy* creepy.

5) *Willard* (2003): Sometimes it's all about the cast. The original *Willard*, made in 1971, has not aged well at all over the past three decades, so merely updating the story wouldn't have been enough to make director Glen Morgan's remake a better film. What made Glen Morgan's remake an instant, if unheralded, classic upon its release were the deliriously wonderful performances by the iconic character actors R. Lee Ermy and Crispin Glover. Casting the infamously eccentric Glover as the rat-loving title character would be enough to earn the film a cult reputation, but the film itself is extremely well shot and successfully walks a very fine line between comedy, horror and pathos. As an added bonus Glover sings "Ben," the Oscar-nominated(!) Michael Jackson-penned title song from the original's 1972 sequel, over the closing credits, which itself is worth the price of admission.

"Turn that off!" (Naomi Watts and David Dorfman in *The Ring*)

The Not-So-Good

Making a remake is a very tricky proposition because it is based on the assumption that it is possible to catch lightning in a bottle more than once. Often the quality that makes a movie great is so indefinable that it cannot be recaptured simply by telling the same story over again. The lesson learned by the filmmakers responsible for the five films mentioned below is that the danger of trying to recapture a great film's lightning is that you can end up very badly burned.

1) *Psycho* (1998): I honestly admire the chutzpah it took for director Gus Van Sant and producer Brian Grazer to even attempt a shot-for-shot remake of Alfred Hitchcock's most influential and arguably greatest film, if only because the result proves that you can take a great cast and a great director and have them work with a slightly updated version of the original script and still fail to recreate another film's greatness. What then is missing in this detailed recreation of the original? Anthony Perkins. With all apologies to Mr. Hitchcock and his famous shower scene, I believe it is Perkins' performance as Norman Bates that has made the 1960 original the enduring classic that it is today, and as good as Vince Vaughn is, in this instance he simply couldn't measure up.

2) *The Bride* (1985): One of the reasons many remakes fail is because their filmmakers have mistakenly assumed that what made the first film great was its story and not how the story was told. This is definitely the case of *The Bride*, a mid-1980s remake of James Whale's classic *Bride of Frankenstein*, which forsakes the original's deliberately campy charm and replaces it with a humorless dramatic tone that only highlights rather than alleviates the story's implausibilities. Paced and directed like a Victorian costume drama, the film actually expects the audience to take the story seriously and the result is agonizing to watch, especially whenever Jennifer Beals, hot off the success of *Flashdance* (1983), is on screen as the title character.

3) *Carnival of Souls* **(1998):** Officially released as *Wes Craven Presents Carnival of Souls,* this remake of Herc Harvey's 1962 cult classic was produced, but not directed, by the famous horror director whose name was so carefully included in the title. Essentially released direct-to-video, this low-budget effort is so incompetently put together that it barely resembles a movie, much less a remake of an extremely influential and atmospheric classic. The film is slightly redeemed by a moving performance by B-movie stalwart Bobbie Phillips (*Showgirls* (1995), TV's *Murder One* and the popular insect episode of *The X-Files*) as the movie's heroine, but the quality of her performance only really succeeds in highlighting how awful the rest of the film really is.

4) *Night of the Living Dead* **(1990):** Originally, George Romero intended to direct this remake of his own 1968 film, but other commitments and a need to get the film made before the rights to the original fell into the public domain forced him to hand over the reigns to Tom Savini, a make-up and special effects artist whose gory work in dozens of scary movies has earned him a loyal following among horror aficionados. But, as films directed by other notable effects technicians such as Stan Winston (*Pumpkinhead*) and Chris

Walas (*The Fly II*) proved, the ability to create gore doesn't necessarily translate into the ability to direct it.

5) *Dracula* (1979): While one can quibble over whether or not a film based on a book that has already been adapted countless times counts as a remake, one thing is certain: John Badham's follow-up to his hugely successful *Saturday Night Fever* (1977) was a massive letdown. Based on a stage play that took many liberties with Bram Stoker's text (including turning the character of Mina Harker into Mina Van Helsing), Badham made the mistake of casting the play's lead, Frank Langella, in the title role. Normally a great actor, Langella looks far too contemporary to play the count. Also doing the film a disservice is Laurence Olivier, whose embodiment of Dr. Van Helsing is another notch in his record for the greatest number of horrible performances ever given by a highly respected actor (a title for which he has drawn fierce competition from actors such as Richard Burton, Marlon Brando and Al Pacino). Still, considering how poorly the 1931 adaptation starring Bela Lugosi has aged over the years, this is the only film in this list that actually manages to be more fun to watch than the original, if only just barely.

6

Groovy!

Evil Dead II: Dead By Dawn

This has easily been the worst weekend getaway of Ash's life.

He's been forced to kill and bury his girlfriend Linda
after she became possessed by the evil spirit of a Kandarian
demon,
only to be possessed himself,
thrown through the windshield of a car,
watch Linda's headless zombie as it performs an interpretive
dance.
He cut up her body with a chainsaw,
cut off his own left hand after it became possessed,
and gets mocked by the cabin's inanimate objects,
attacked by his own dismembered hand,
beaten up by an inbred local,
thrown down into a cellar with a very ugly and very dead old
woman.
He is possessed once again,
almost killed with an ax,
forced to go back into the cellar to find the missing pages
that contain the spells that will stop the demons,
and then attacked by living trees and a gigantic Kandarian
demon
before finally being sucked into the 14th century by a swirling
mystical time warp.

And you thought you've had bad vacations...

A Bloody Great Time

That's right! Who's laughing now?
—Ash (Bruce Campbell), *Evil Dead II: Dead By Dawn*

There's no question that most movie sequels end up being inferior to the films that came before them (in other words, they suck.) Such monumental disappointments such as *Psycho II* (1983), *Halloween II* (1981), *A Nightmare On Elm Street Part 2: Freddy's Revenge* (1985) and *The Fly II* (1989) are just a few examples of horrible sequels made after some of the great films discussed in this book. But there are, of course, exceptions to every rule, and sometimes a group of film-makers are able to make a sequel that not only equals the original, but actually surpasses it as well. The best example of this rare phenomenon is Sam Raimi's cult masterpiece *Evil Dead II: Dead By Dawn* (1987). Not only is it a better film than the first *Evil Dead*, it is also one of the most hilarious and entertaining horror rides of all time.

To give you just a small sense of what I mean, look again at the line of dialogue quoted above. It doesn't seem to be anything special does it? One could even call it cliché if one were in a mood to do so. But now imagine it as it appears in the movie, as the film's hapless protagonist shouts it at his own left hand—which has become possessed by a demon—as he cuts off the homicidal appendage with a chainsaw. After the hand has been successfully amputated, the hero covers it with a wastepaper basket, which he weighs down with some nearby books. The camera makes sure to catch the title of the book on the top of the pile—Ernest Hemingway's *A Farewell to Arms.*

If you don't immediately understand what makes this such a great sequence (and are somewhat appalled by the very idea of it) then this is not the film for you, because what I have just described is actually one of *Evil Dead II*'s subtlest moments. This is a film for which the term over-the-top is wholly inadequate. It goes so far beyond the normal standards of a conventional horror film and approaches the anything-goes style of a live-action Warner Brothers cartoon (albeit one with *a lot* more blood than Bugs, Daffy and Elmer ever had to deal with). But the miracle of this film is that this cartoonish quality does not diminish the film's horrific thrills, but instead only makes them that much more intense. Similar to John Landis' *An American Werewolf in London* (1981), the film's humor is not kept separate from its horror, so the viewer is often compelled to laugh and scream at the same time. The result of this is one of the most exhilarating experiences in all of scary movie history.

Any attempt to dwell for even a second on what the film "means" leaves a person feeling both foolish and achingly pretentious. This is a film that is all about action and madness and was never intended to be insightful. While some people may be annoyed or troubled by this deliberate lack of depth, they are forgetting the pure joy that can come from simply being entertained.

How It Happened

Given the almost dementedly juvenile glee that pervades throughout the film, it isn't at all surprising to discover that its origin goes all the way back to a group of teenaged boys in junior high school. West Maple Junior High School, located in a small suburb of Detroit, Michigan, is where Bruce Campbell, a young wannabe actor, met up with a couple of Three Stooges enthusiasts named Scott Spiegel and Sam Raimi. Along with their friends (which included another future director named Josh Becker,)[1] this energetic trio produced a series of home movies of simple slapstick, which titles included *Inspector Klutz Saves the Day*, *Three Pests in a Mess* and *The Singing Nuts*.

Unlike other budding filmmakers who eventually grew tired of playing with their father's 8 mm cameras, Campbell, Spiegel and Raimi's cinematic ambitions became more elaborate and complicated, involving period costumes for WWII films and a car chase for a James Bond parody. It wasn't until Raimi wrote and directed a film by himself called *The Happy Valley Kid* that they realized that filmmaking could also be a viable way to earn a living.

Raimi made the film when he was attending Michigan State University in 1978. When his brother Ivan[2] became unavailable to play the lead, he cast Ivan's dormmate, Rob Tappert, in the title role. Having spent $700 to make the film, Raimi decided to recoup his investment by showing the film

---

1 His films include *Thou Shalt Not Kill, Except...* (1985) and *Running Time* (1997).

2 Now a successful surgeon who has occasionally moonlighted away from medicine to co-write such films as *Darkman* (1990) and *Army of Darkness* (1993).

on campus, charging $1.50 a ticket. It proved to be such a popular hit that it eventually grossed $5,000 at the box office. Though that doesn't sound like much, it meant that the film had taken in over six times what it had cost, which is a cost-to-profit ratio every producer and executive in Hollywood would ~~kill~~ love to achieve just once in their career.

After Raimi's success, the original group reunited to make their biggest film yet, *It's Murder*. Unfortunately, lightning didn't strike twice. The $2,000 epic failed to appeal to audiences like *The Happy Valley Kid* had, and it did not make a profit. Noting that the only scene anyone seemed to enjoy from their flop was a scary moment in which a killer suddenly appears from the back seat of a car, they decided that their next effort would be an unrelenting horror movie.

This time, they planned to make a film good enough to earn national distribution. They decided to look for local businessmen to finance their movie. Joined by Rob Tappert, they decided that the best way to get the attention of potential investors would be to make a short film that proved they knew what they were doing. The result was the 30-minute film, *Within the Woods* (1978), which cost $1,600 and served as a template for the first two *Evil Dead* films. Despite its slightly amateurish quality, the film was effective enough to get the money they needed.

The working title of their first "real" film was *Book of the Dead*, a story of a group of five college kids who gather together to spend the weekend at an old, abandoned cabin in the woods. Unfortunately for them, the cabin was last occupied by a professor who had spent his career studying the ancient civilization of Kandar. Among the artifacts he had brought with him was the Kandarian *Necronomicon Ex Mortis* (Book of the Dead), a book bound with the skin of a man's face and written in blood. The two men in the group, Ash (Bruce Campbell) and Scotty[3] (Rich Demanicor, acting under the pseudonym Hal Delrich),[4] discover the book, along with a sinister-looking dagger and a tape recorder in the cabin's cellar. Curious, the five of them listen to a reel-to-reel recording of the professor reading from the Book of the Dead. What they do not know is that speaking aloud the words written in the Book of the Dead has the effect of raising up a dark and evil spirit that lives in the forest. Only one of the five friends survive the night and even his fate is in question at the end.

With Raimi directing, Tappert producing and Campbell playing the lead role, production on *Book of the Dead* began on November 14, 1979, and finished two and a half months later. Having spent the $85,000 they had initially earned to make the film, they had to go back to their investors for more money. Luckily they got what they needed and the post-production began. Tom Sullivan, the man who had designed the Book of the Dead and the Kandarian dagger—along with Bart Piece—was given the go-ahead to create the film's final special effects sequence. The two men created the unforgettably

---

3 This character was named after Scott Spiegel, who basically played the same part in *Within the Woods*. He wasn't able to join his friends when they went on to make the *Book of the Dead*, but he eventually helped them during post-production and would eventually cowrite *Evil Dead II*.

4 Demanicor chose to use a pseudonym in the credits of the movie not because he was ashamed to be in a low-budget horror movie, but because he was a member of the Screen Actors Guild and was appearing in the film for less than the guild's minimum wage. He created the alias by combining his name with his roommates, Hal and Del.

repulsive deadite[5] meltdown finale using a combination of stop-motion animation and mechanical effects.

After the effects were finished and all of the reshoots and pickup shots were completed, they handed their negatives to Edna Ruth Paul, a New York editor whose previous experience was mostly limited to episodes of the popular *ABC Afterschool Special.* Her assistant was a young man named Joel Coen, who became good friends with Raimi and who later—along with his brother Ethan—would go on to direct the films *Raising Arizona* (1987), *Fargo* (1996) and *The Big Lebowski* (1998). A composer named Joseph LoDuca was hired to write the film's score and months passed as the film edged closer and closer to completion. The film premiered on October 15, 1981, at Detroit's Redford Theater.

Even those who had some idea of what was coming weren't prepared for what they saw in the film. Unlike most directors working with such a limited budget, Raimi was able to avoid the use of simple, static takes and to create tension through creative movement of his camera. One of Raimi's impressive innovations was how he was able to give the evil spirit in the forest a powerful presence thanks to a device that was invented for the film called the Shakeycam. The Shakeycam consisted of a camera tied in the middle of a board of wood. The effect was similar to that of the more professional Steadicam, a device that allows for steady, fluid movement of the camera without the use of cumbersome dolly tracks. This more primitive device succeeded in giving the spirit's point of view a power and a personality that would have been impossible using more traditional methods.

---

5 The name given to all of the demons who appear in the *Evil Dead* films.

What was even more shocking than *Book of the Dead*'s technical achievements was the film's sadistic cruelty towards its characters. It's hard to think of a film that preceded it in which the protagonists suffered more. Much of the film's terror comes from the fact that these people were victims of circumstance whose curiosity about a tape recording led to their ultimate fate. The evil spirit possessed the victim's body *and* soul. The punishment for being in this wrong place at this wrong time is not merely death, but eternal damnation. The idea that good and normal people—thanks to a random twist of fate—can be doomed to suffer torments they do not deserve is a common theme in horror movies, but few films have ever used it as effectively as it is here.

It also didn't hurt that Raimi and his cohorts gleefully ignored the old horror rule that less is more and decided to make a film where more *wasn't enough*. Though there are some traditional moments of suspense early on in the film, they are soon passed over in favor of an onslaught of direct and graphic imagery. Instead of following the path set by *Psycho* (1960), *The Texas Chainsaw Massacre* (1974) and *Halloween* (1978), where the violence is kept to a minimum and mostly suggested but not shown, *Book of the Dead* showed *everything*. The effect is unsettling, especially as the acts committed in the film get more and more extreme. By the time Ash has been taunted by the disembodied head of his deadite girlfriend, Linda (Betsy Baker), it becomes impossible to imagine how things could get any worse. And then they do.

In the end what the audience at the Redford Theater was so unprepared to take was the film's unrelenting grimness. *Book of the Dead* was a film without much humor or any

When Sam Raimi went to see Wes Craven's *The Hills Have Eyes* (1977), he noticed that in one scene Craven had placed a torn-up poster for Steven Spielberg's *Jaws* (1975) on a wall. Raimi interpreted this to mean that Craven was making a subtle comment about Spielberg's blockbuster, suggesting that its mechanical shark was nowhere near as terrifying as *Eyes* feral family of desert cannibals. Raimi decided to one-up Craven and included a torn-up poster for *Eyes* on the wall of the cabin's cellar in *The Evil Dead*, thus signifying that his monsters were much more frightening than Craven's. This did not go unnoticed and Craven included a scene in *A Nightmare On Elm Street* in which Nancy, the film's young heroine, struggles to stay awake by watching *The Evil Dead* on TV. The implication being that watching the horrors inflicted on Ash and his friends was much more preferable than being caught in a nightmare with Freddy Krueger.

hope. There were no moments of levity to ease the tension and there was no happy ending where the demons have been vanquished and life can go on. The film's final scene is a Shakeycam shot that represented the evil spirit in the forest. It speeds through the cabin and out the door towards a screaming Ash, possessing him as the image fades and the credits start. Even the hero doesn't make it.

Given the film's inherent bleakness, it is no surprise then that when Renaissance Pictures[6] tried to find a distributor for it, they were turned down by almost everyone. The only distributor who was at all interested was Robert Shaye's New

---

6 The production company Rob and Sam formed to produce their movie.

Line Cinema. Though the company would later go on to bigger things thanks to their Freddy Krueger franchise (and then on to enormous things when it produced Peter Jackson's blockbuster *Lord of the Rings* trilogy), they were a very small company at the time whose biggest success was John Waters' infamous *Pink Flamingos* (1972). They offered to distribute the film for Renaissance, but they refused to advance the company a single dollar. Raimi and Tappert decided to look elsewhere.

Their luck finally changed when they screened the film for a well-known Hollywood businessman named Irvin Shapiro. In his 70s at the time, Irvin's dealings with horror films went all the way back to the 1920s when he played a role in getting the German classic *The Cabinet of Dr. Caligari* (1920) distributed in North America. He felt that money could be made from *Book of the Dead*, but he insisted that the title be changed to *The Evil Dead Men and the Evil Dead Women*. Other titles considered were the highly apt *Blood Flood* and the even more unlikely *These Bitches Are Witches*. Eventually, Shapiro's suggestion was refined to *The Evil Dead* (1981).

Shapiro ended up going back to New Line and got a much better deal for Renaissance. He also urged the young film-makers to screen the movie at all of the European film festivals. They took his advice and showed the film at 1982's Cannes Film Festival, the most important film festival in the world. Luckily for them, Stephen King, the legendary horror novelist, saw the film there and was blown away by it. He wrote an enthusiastic review for the film for *Twilight Zone* magazine. Word of the movie began to spread and by the time it was released in the United States in April 1983, it was well known enough to become a cult hit with horror fans, but it still took six years for the film to turn a profit for Renaissance Pictures.

The attention Raimi received allowed him to get financing for his second film, *Crimewave* (1985), which was similar to the screwball, slapstick comedies that he, Campbell and Spiegel had made as kids. Cowritten by Raimi, and Joel and Ethan Coen, the film was meant to echo the style of the comedies from the 1930s and 1940s.[7] But the film's financiers didn't see eye to eye with Raimi's vision and forced him to make several compromises that hurt the film, the main concession being that Raimi wanted to cast Campbell as the film's lead character, Vic Ajax, but Raimi was forced to cast an actor named Reed Birney[8] in the role instead. When the film was released in 1985, it was a huge flop and the guys at Renaissance Pictures were afraid that their film careers were over.

And so, as is the case with most sequels, the company decided to return to their past success simply because they knew—after the commercial and artistic disappointment of *Crimewave*—it stood as their best chance to revive their flagging careers. Often it is difficult for a filmmaker to return to a project with the same initial enthusiasm. Wes Craven only made the uninspired sequel to *The Hills Have Eyes* because

---

7 The admiration these three have for these comedies must be palpable, because—despite the failure of *Crimewave*—they wrote another film called *The Hudsucker Proxy* (1994) that evoked the style of the exact same period. This time, however, the Coens took control of the directing duties and the result was another financial flop, but the film itself remains one of the Coens' best and most under-appreciated films.

8 Don't worry if you haven't heard of him. His film career after *Crimewave* has been negligible. Chances are if the film had starred Bruce Campbell, the cult success of the *Evil Dead* films would have made it much better known today and might have even allowed it to eventually turn a slim profit.

he was broke and couldn't get any of his other films produced. The same can be said for Tobe Hooper's sequel to
The Texas Chainsaw Massacre, which avoided the terror of the
original in the favor of a not very funny self-parody.

While none of the major players involved in the sequel to
The Evil Dead felt this kind of antipathy for the project, they
did agree that the film should be different from the first. It
was decided that the first film's biggest flaw was its lack of
humor, so they agreed that the sequel would not take itself
as seriously.

Raimi's original conception for the sequel's plot was a
medieval epic involving knights battling deadites in the 13th
century, but this was ultimately rejected as being too ambitious for a sequel to a film that made a modest amount of
money. Raimi went back to the drawing board and recruited
his old friend Scott Spiegel to collaborate on the screenplay,
which resembled more of a remake than a sequel. Due to
rights issues they could not use any footage from the first
film, so all references to it would have to be recreated. The
plan was to reshoot scenes featuring all five of the original
characters, but eventually three of the characters were cut
and the film opened with just Ash and his girlfriend Linda at
the cabin.[9]

The filmmakers decided that the events of the first film
would be replayed in the sequel's first 10 minutes for a
unique experience where virtually no time is spent building

---

9 This decision has irked some fans of the series for taking liberties with the details of the first
film and also for the way this revision indirectly suggests that Ash somehow survived the
first film and got away, but was dumb enough to return to the cabin. This interpretation of
events was aided by the fact that a new actress, Denise Bixler, was cast as Linda, thus suggesting she was a different Linda than the one in the original.

up any tension or developing any kind of characterization. Seven and a half minutes into the film, Ash's girlfriend has already been possessed, decapitated and buried under ground. This willful turn against the standard horror convention of slowly building the terror would eventually prove to be a very smart choice on Raimi and Spiegel's part.

By a strange coincidence, it was Stephen King, who had helped the first film[10] with a rave review, who helped the filmmakers get financing for the sequel. At the time, King was directing his first film, *Maximum Overdrive* (1986), which was being produced by the famed Italian producer Dino De Laurentiis. By chance he heard that Renaissance was looking for money to make *Evil Dead II*, so he went to De Laurentiis and told him that he should produce the movie. A producer who never met a dollar he didn't like, De Laurentiis saw the financial benefits of making the film and agreed. The filmmakers decided to film in Wadesboro, which was in the same state as De Laurentiis Entertainment Group (DEG) offices, but still far enough away that it was unlikely any DEG executives would show up and interfere with or question any of Renaissance's decisions.

The set for the interior of the cabin was built in the gymnasium of the local junior high school[11] and the exteriors were shot in Wadesboro's Blue Ridge Mountains. In replicating the cabin, the art department, headed by Randy Bennet and Phillip Duffin, took a cue from *The Cabinet of Dr. Caligari* and built a set that was deliberately off-balance and

---

10 And presumably last...

11 Which seems apt, considering where Raimi, Spiegel and Campbell originally met each other.

If the blood in *Evil Dead II* looks strange to you, you're very observant. Renaissance's contract with DEG required them to deliver an R-rated film, so they naively decided to change the color of the blood in the hopes that the ratings board would be more lenient on them. Depending on who (or what) is being killed in the film, the color of the blood ranges from black to green to pink to purple. In the end Raimi realized that there was no way his final cut could ever get an R-rating, so he didn't even bother showing the film to the ratings board. Instead, DEG formed a one-time only company called Rosebud Releasing Corporation and released the film to theaters unrated.

askew, suggesting the madness that Ash finds himself battling as the demons try to kill him. Also lifted from the famous, German silent film was a possible ending in which it turns out that Ash is really insane and has merely hallucinated everything that has happened to him.

To film the movie they hired a young cinematographer with little experience named Peter Deming,[12] and to create the film's many demons[13] and bloody effects they hired another neophyte named Greg Nicotero.[14] Joseph LoDuca also returned from the original to compose the film's score.

---

12 He would later go on to shoot *My Cousin Vinny* (1992), ~~Scream 2~~ & *3* and *Austin Powers: International Man of Mystery* (1997).

13 Ash's deadite makeup was partly inspired by the character of Witchiepoo from the 1970's Sid and Marty Krofft TV show *H.R. Pufnstuf*.

14 His company KNB, cofounded with Howard Berger and Robert Kurtzman, would go on to do the effects for many Hollywood movies, including both volumes of *Kill Bill* (2003, 2004) and *Minority Report* (2002).

The small cast was filled with inexpensive, unknown actors and production began in the middle of 1986.

Production on the film went much easier than it had during the first movie. The only people who really suffered were Ted Raimi[15] and Bruce Campbell. Of the two of them, Campbell got it the worst.[16] Because Ash spent so much of the film drenched in blood, Bruce found himself constantly covered with the thick and sweet red syrup used as his makeup. Flies loved it and followed him wherever he went, and it proved virtually impossible to remove when he was off the set. Also, Raimi's complicated setups would test Campbell's physical abilities. During the filming of one shot, which required the film to be shot backwards, Raimi lost his patience with his star and told him that that "...was the worst reverse motion acting I have ever seen!" But Campbell's devotion to the film never wavered. Scott Spiegel suggested that even if Raimi asked Campbell to jump off a roof and land on his neck, Campbell would not only do it, he would do it in character.

When the film was released, the critics liked the film, the public didn't. The film flopped during its initial run in theaters, and only did okay on home video. The film did much better internationally, where it was a huge hit in Italy and

---

15 The suit Sam's younger brother had to wear as the deadite hag Henrietta was so hot that if you watch closely during the scene where he attacks Annie you can see a trickle of sweat pour out of his costume. It happens during the 1h 11m 51s mark of the movie's runtime.

16 It says something about the cartoonish style of the *Evil Dead II* that the only act of violence cut out of the film by the British film censors is the moment where Jake kicks Ash in the face while he lies nearly unconscious on the floor. The censors apparently had no problem with the film's many instances of dismemberment or decapitation, but they weren't going to let the filmmakers get away with someone kicking the hero while he's down.

Depending on your taste, one of the funniest scenes in the movie involves the somewhat simple character of Bobbie Joe. In it, Ash and Bobbie Joe's boyfriend, Jake, hit the deadite hag Henrietta so hard with the basement's trapdoor that one of the demon's eyes pops out of its socket and flies into Bobbie Joe's screaming mouth. What makes this Three-Stooges inspired gag even more interesting to watch is the fact that the role of Bobbie Joe was originally written for the actress Holly Hunter, who was living in the house Sam Raimi shared with the Coen brothers while he and Scott Spiegel were working on the script. While Spiegel has claimed that the reason she wasn't cast in the part was because Rob Tappert wanted a more typically sexy actress for the role, Tappert has insisted that by 1986 Hunter had already been cast in *Raising Arizona* and was well on her way to a serious acting career, making it unlikely she would have accepted the role even if it had been offered to her.

Japan. As the years went by, the cult surrounding the film began to grow. In 1993 the editors of *Spin* magazine declared it the best movie that had been released since the magazine had started publication in 1985. Since then the film's reputation has grown exponentially and is now considered one of the true modern classics of the genre.[17]

---

17 Its status as a true cult classic was confirmed when, in 2003, the film was turned into a popular stage musical by a theater group in Toronto, Canada.

The Aftermath

Despite the film's initial failure, Dino De Laurentiis agreed to produce another sequel. *Evil Dead III* (eventually retitled *Army of Darkness*) was the movie Raimi wanted to make originally instead of *Evil Dead II*. It started where the second film left off, with Ash stranded in another time and forced to continue his fight with the deadites. The film was much less violent than its predecessors and was closer in spirit to classic Saturday afternoon matinee adventures such as *Jason and the Argonauts* and *The Seventh Voyage of Sinbad* than it was to a typical horror film. Like the first three films it didn't do well theatrically, but did well on video, and its reputation has grown dramatically over the years. It has become the most heavily licensed of the films and a trip to any comic-book store will yield a surprising array of Ash-inspired products.

After making the comic-book movie *Darkman*, which proceeded *Army of Darkness*, Raimi and Tappert went into television and produced the successful, syndicated action-adventure comedies *Hercules: The Legendary Journeys* and *Xena: Warrior Princess*. Raimi then directed a western called *The Quick and the Dead* (1995) that starred Sharon Stone as a female gunfighter looking to kill the man who ruined her childhood. He followed that up with two movies that proved he could make films that did not depend on fancy camera tricks or any other typically "Raimi-esque" touches. *A Simple Plan* (1998) was the story of a group of men who find a briefcase full of stolen money and how it ruins their lives, and *For the Love of the Game* (1999) was about a baseball player who finds himself thinking about his relationships with his loved ones while he pitches a perfect game. Critics were surprised by *A Simple Plan*, which was one of the most powerful and moving dramas of 1998.[18] It proved that Sam Raimi could do serious work as well as any other well-respected director. He then made a welcome return to his horror movie roots with the gothic ghost story *The Gift* (2000).

The Gift is about as far from *Evil Dead II* as any scary movie can get. Closer in style to *A Simple Plan*, it told the story of a widowed psychic (Cate Blanchett) who is tormented by visions of a young woman's murder. Once again, Raimi proved that he was more talented than people first realized.

For years James Cameron, the director of *The Terminator* (1984) and *True Lies* (1994), tried to make a feature version of the popular Spider-Man comic book, but the rights to the character were tied up in complicated litigation that made it unlikely the film would ever get made. By the time the film rights did become available, Cameron had made *Titanic* (1997), the most successful film of all time, and was no longer interested in the Spider-Man character. The search went out for a director to make the film that had been hotly anticipated by the public for close to a decade. When Sam Raimi's name came up as a possibility, it was his work on the *Evil Dead* movies that got the producers interested. In the end he got the job and has thus far delivered two films that have managed to excite the public and please the critics. With *Spider-Man II* (2004), he has become that rare director who has been able to make not one, but two sequels that improved upon the original.

---

18 Driven as it was by an amazing Academy Award-nominated performance by Billy Bob Thornton as the pathetic Jacob Morton.

Also Look For

Anchor Bay Entertainment have released several editions of the *Evil Dead* movies on video and DVD over the years, but the ones that I recommend are the special-limited editions of the first two films. The coolest is the *Book of the Dead* edition of the first film, which was packaged in a rubber replica of the *Necronomicom Ex Mortis*. A tin-case edition of the second film was also released. Both films include great commentaries by the cast and crew, as well as several interesting documentaries. Regular issues of both films are available, but the collector editions mentioned above can still be found. And if you're interested in reading more about these movies than you should pick up Bill Warren's *The Evil Dead Companion*, which is a well-written account of how the films got made. Even more entertaining is Bruce Campbell's autobiography *If Chins Could Kill: Confessions of a B-Movie Actor*. It's a very funny book that details the adventures of a man who has made a living starring in low-budget films and getting small parts in more mainstream Hollywood fare.

Scared Again

The Good

Evil Dead II is a real scary movie rarity, but it's not the only horror movie sequel that is as good or even better than the original. Here are five more to look out for.

1) *Aliens* **(1986):** James Cameron's sequel to Ridley Scott's classic is not only as exciting as the first film, it also gives Sigourney Weaver's character Ripley the substance she lacked in the original.

2) *Bride of Frankenstein* **(1935):** James Whale's follow-up to his classic *Frankenstein* improved upon the original thanks to his daring use of deliberate campy humor.

3) *Bride of Chucky* **(1998):** Considering how bad the first three *Child's Play* movies were, this third sequel in the series only had to be watchable in order to be an improvement. But thanks to some playful direction by Ronny Yu, a fun script by Don Mancini and a great performance by Jennifer Tilly, this film is actually far more entertaining than it has any right to be.

4) *Return of the Living Dead III* **(1993):** Director Brian Yuzna and screenwriter John Penney bring an emotional quality not previously seen in this series by turning it into a zombie version of *Romeo and Juliet*. Actress Melinda Clarke

Another plastic surgery disaster.
(Elsa Lanchester in *The Bride of Frankenstein*)

(who is best known today for playing a sexy mom on *The OC*) creates genuine pathos in her role as a young woman who fights against her cannibalistic impulses after being turned into a zombie by her grieving boyfriend.

The blood-spattered bride doll. (Tiffany in *Bride of Chucky*)

5) *Wes Craven's New Nightmare* **(1994):** Two years before his career was revived with the success of the postmodern slasher movie *Scream*, Wes Craven made this even more interesting sequel to his *A Nightmare On Elm Street*. In it, the men and women who made that classic film find themselves tormented by the evil demon who inspired the character of Freddy Krueger and find that they can only stop him by making yet another sequel in the long franchise.

The Not-So-Good

Now that you know of some sequels to look for, here are five that you should avoid like the plague.

1) *The Exorcist II: The Heretic* **(1977):** Personally I think William Friedkin's *The Exorcist* (1973) is the single most overrated horror film of all time, but even it deserved better than this. It is a mystical mumbo-jumbo that at times seemed to be designed as a cure for the very worst case of insomnia.

2) *Jaws: The Revenge* **(1987):** The tagline for this film actually read "This Time It's Personal..." Personal for *the shark*! Not since Richard Harris dueled it out with *Orca: Killer Whale* (1977) has an aquatic revenge tale been so completely misguided. This film represents a nautical disaster so severe it makes *Jaws 3-D* (1983) look like *Moby Dick*. No, strike that. It's so bad it makes *Jaws 3-D* look like *Jaws* (1975) itself. Do not go into this water. You have been warned.

The terror of the deep. (The shark in *Jaws: The Revenge*)

3) ***Book of Shadows: Blair Witch II*** **(2000):** Considering the enormous success of the first film, it's no wonder Artisan Entertainment rushed this film into production, planning it to be the first in a long line of *Blair Witch* movies. Unfortunately, what they failed to realize was that the popularity of the first film had more to do with its amazing marketing campaign and less to do with its actual entertainment value, and people had absolutely no interest in seeing the story continue. This sequel succeeds in being even more boring than the first movie was.

4) ***The Boogeyman II/Silent Night, Deadly Night II*** **(1983/1987):** These two films have the undesirable distinction of not only being sequels to bad movies, but also being films that are almost entirely made with flashbacks featuring scenes from the terrible originals. Insult + Injury = Not a fun time for the audience. At least when Wes Craven did this in *The Hills Have Eyes II,* he had the sense of humor to show one of the flashbacks from a dog's perspective.

5) ***AVP: Aliens Vs. Predator*** **(2004):** This movie serves as a warning to geeks everywhere: be careful what you wish for, because you just might get it. Genre fanatics everywhere salivated at the thought of combining these two series into one kick-ass motion picture, thanks entirely to a "don't-blink-or-you'll-miss-it" inside joke that appeared in *Predator 2* (1990). In the film, fans were teased with a brief shot of the Predator's collection of hunting trophies, one of which appeared to be the skull of an Alien. This split-second reference resulted in a comic book series, video games and a famous spec script[1] by Peter Briggs[2] that was widely distributed over the Internet.

For over a decade, geeks dreamed of the day when this film would be released, but the poor box office performance of *Alien: Ressurection* (1997), the fourth film in the *Alien* series, did little to convince 20th Century Fox to make it. Then, in 2003, when New Line had a huge hit with *Freddy Vs. Jason*,[3] the executives at Fox took notice. After languishing for years in development, *Alien Vs. Predator* was fast tracked into production. Unfortunately for Peter Briggs, his popular script was the first thing to go, mainly because it had become so ubiquitous on the Internet that the studio figured it would hold no surprises for its core audience. Needing to get the movie done as soon as they could, the executives in charge hired director Paul W.S. Anderson,[4] who had a reputation for making big movies with mid-size budgets. Unfortunately for fans, the reason Anderson was able to get movies such as *Mortal Kombat* (1995) and *Resident Evil* (2002) made for such low budgets was because he didn't seem to care if they were any good or not. *AVP* was made in time for its release date and with a reasonable budget, but it wasn't worth watching.

---

1 A spec script is a screenplay written by a screenwriter for no money, with the assumption that they will be able to sell it to a producer or studio when it is finished.

2 Who would later make significant contributions to the script for Guillermo Del Toro's comic-book adaption *Hellboy* (2004).

3 Which, as you read in the chapter on *A Nightmare On Elm Street*, had an almost identical genesis as *AVP*.

4 Not to be confused with Paul Thomas Anderson (aka P.T. Anderson), the director of *Boogie Nights* (1997) and *Magnolia* (1999).

Can you believe they waited that long for this?
(An Alien and a Predator in *AVP: Alien Vs. Predator*)

In all fairness, though, this was a project doomed in its conception. As much as the premise entranced its fans' imaginations, it suffered from the problem that both the Aliens and the Predators were inhuman, unsympathetic creatures devoted to killing, which provided little for an audience to care about. Anderson's film introduced human characters into the mix, but they only made the problem worse, thanks to a predictable script and poor performances by the actors. Despite all its failings, and thanks to the years of pent-up demand for the project, *AVP* was a hit when it came out, which means that a (conceivably) even worse sequel is in the works as these words are being written.

Add To Your Ghost House Collection With These New Titles Full of Fascinating Mysteries and Terrifying Tales.

Scary Stories
by Andrew Warwick

A fun collection of creepy tales, from twisted urban legends and laugh-out-loud absurditie to paranormal phenomena. Three men stranded by a scheming tour guide find out wh their destination is called "Cannibal Falls." Having died of shame thanks to a bell tie around its neck, a cat's bitter spirit seeks revenge on its owner. A selfish American business man acquires a mummy with a haunted past—and pays the price for his greed. And muc more!

$10.95USD/$14.95CDN • ISBN 1-894877-61-6 • 5.25" x 8.25" • 224 pages

Premonitions and Psychic Warnings
by Edrick Thay

Since the dawn of time, people have experienced premonitions. Some foretell disaster while others help to prevent them. A soldier who can smell emotions and see death help his troop avoid a military ambush in the jungle. On a prairie highway, a woman encounte an eyeless hitchhiker who bears more than a passing resemblance to her ailing aunt. vision of twisted metal and broken glass saves a reckless girl from a car accident. These a just some of the eyewitness accounts explored by author Edrick Thay as he studies th remarkable effects of superhuman perception on the lives of ordinary people.

$10.95USD/$14.95CDN • ISBN 1-894877-58-6 • 5.25" x 8.25" • 232 pages

Famous People of the Paranormal
by Chris Wangler

Shamans, psychics, yogis, channelers—almost every culture singles out people with extrao dinary gifts. This ambitious book explores the bizarre lives of paranormal celebriti through the ages. As you might imagine, not everyone in this unusual field is genuin author Chris Wangler also exposes a handful of bona fide paranormal charlatans.

$10.95USD/$14.95CDN • ISBN 1-894877-45-4 • 5.25" x 8.25" • 240 pages

These and many more Ghost House books are available from your local bookseller or ordering direct. U.S. readers call 1-800-518-3541. In Canada, call 1-800-661-9017.